ACKN(

Although I am not th
my brother Chris, I an.
lost in the Bermuda Triangle.

This was my first attempt in this field and without the help and encouragement of the people listed below I would never have achieved it.

The first editor Nina F. Ryan, whose task was not easy, had to work from a very rough draft written by a non-native English speaker.

The copy editor, Robert Brill, whose knowledge of the sea and keen interest in this book was a great help to me.

Rey Hernandez, the graphic designer, worked closely with me to change and incorporate the constant changes.

The above were the professionals – now to the others:

My cousin, Felicity Yost, who as a writer and graphic designer for the United Nations in New York City, was a major influence in this project and never let me slack off!

My cousin, Marek Zgorniak, an art historian in Krakow, Poland, whose keen eye and knowledge of publishing, was an outstanding asset.

Danielle Bastarache, who is a Real Estate professional and has collaborated on publishing two books and shared her knowledge and experience.

I also want to thank my family and the friends who read the rough manuscript for telling me how much they enjoyed it which in turn helped me in taking the decision to publish it.

Ken Hahn, thank you for guiding me with the complexities of the computer.

CONTENTS

INTRODUCTION

By Daisy de Grabowski Richardson

My brother, Chris, saw the Baltic Sea for the first time when he was seven years old. From that moment on, the sea became his passion. In 1959 he realized a dream when he completed a solo crossing of the Atlantic from Tangier to New York on his beloved *Tethys*. The twenty-five-foot yacht was aptly named. *Tethys* means Goddess of the Sea in Greek.

This book is my brother's account of his solitary journey across the ocean and his grueling shakedown voyage in the Mediterranean Sea with his twelve-year-old son, Mark, and his friend, Bep. His story, set at sea and in a dozen ports, is a window on soon-to-vanish traces of a just-ended era and on the future at the dawn of a new international alignment. He provides powerful personal insight into the history of sailing and into the spiritual and emotional struggle to prepare himself for the extreme nature of the voyage. During the 84 days of the crossing, he never touched land or communicated with anyone.

Born in Poland, Count Christopher de Grabowski came from a long line of Polish nobles, including many generals. His love for the sea made him the first in the family to aspire to join the Polish navy. In 1938, our father, afraid of the fate that might befall his son in a war he had long foreseen, sent Chris to live with a relative in Chile. The following year, Poland was invaded.

Chris' desire to come to the aid of his country could not be so easily thwarted. He sailed to England in 1941. He volunteered for Bomber Squadron 301, the Polish Wing of the Royal Air Force, rose to the rank of flight lieutenant and was decorated with many medals, including the Distinguished Flying Cross and the Polish Virtuti Militari.

Our father, an engineer by profession, was offered a commission with the British Engineering Corps. Our mother, a gifted painter, joined the British Red Cross as an officer and served as an occupational therapist treating shell-shocked British troops in Gaza, service which earned her the British King's Medal.

As tail gunner in heavy bombers, Chris flew eighty missions over Germany, Italy, Yugoslavia, Greece and Czechoslovakia during World War II. His sorties also took him over Poland during the doomed 1944 Warsaw uprising. He could not have known his future wife was among those Polish fighters.

Chris was fluent in seven languages. After the war, with his command of the English language and talent for photography, he landed a job with the United States Information Agency based at the American Embassy in Tunis. As a public relations officer, he traveled throughout Africa and made several documentary films.

He also devoted much time to sailing, which brought him great joy. He won many trophies and cups racing on the Mediterranean. He became Vice Commodore of the Slocum Society and a member of several exclusive yacht clubs. He wrote about his experiences, and his articles and photographs were published in yachting magazines in Europe and the United States.

In 1957, he was sent for three months of training in the United States. He returned full of admiration for the American spirit. Later, in an article about his Atlantic crossing, he remarked on "the goodness of heart prevailing among Americans" and "high moral value of the principles upon which the American system is based." Ever since Chris had read his first account of a small boat voyage – Alain Gerbault's, "In Quest of the Sun" – the idea of sailing solo across the ocean had lived in his mind. Now another dream emerged: he would immigrate to the United States and become an American citizen.

Between 1957 and 1959, he made several unsuccessful attempts to cross the Atlantic. These efforts prepared him for the voyage which would let him experience the freedom that he called "the greatest gift life can give." In 1958, he purchased

Tethys from Bep Patti, his friend and fellow sailor who had commissioned her from a local Tunisian craftsman, overseen her construction, and sailed this "splendid example of a small deep-seagoing vessel" for ten years.

On Sunday, April 12, 1959, full of trepidation after the difficulties of his preceding Mediterranean voyage from Tunis to Gibraltar, Chris set sail. His log entry at four-twenty p.m. as he passed the outer breakwater of the harbor read: "From Tangier to New York. Wind East, Force 5. Two reefs in main. A most satisfactory departure."

He sailed into New York aboard *Tethys* on the fifth of July and proudly handed over his passport replete with a U.S. Visa granting him entry into the country and starting him on the path to citizenship. This was a dream that for Chris would not come true.

The aftermath of the crossing was as difficult as its beginning leg on the Mediterranean in its spiritual impact, and Chris describes the struggle with depression that followed his solo voyage. By the end of 1959, he and his wife divorced. He never again returned to a life on land.

From 1960 to 1963 Chris served as a Sailing Master on private yachts in the West Indies, and captained the *Yankee Clipper*, a schooner belonging to Windjammer Barefoot Cruises. He also skippered the *Caroline*, a yacht belonging to a woman by the same name whom he hoped to marry.

In the winter of 1964, Chris took a job as skipper of the *Enchantress* bound for Tahiti out of Charleston, South Carolina. Aboard were the owner, a businessman for whom the trip was a lifelong dream, his wife and two young children. The 58-foot, two-masted schooner encountered a hurricane, an unusual occurrence at that time of year.

On Jan. 13, at 4 p.m. the *Enchantress* issued a distress signal from the Bermuda Triangle off the coast of Jacksonville, Florida. At 4:08 the sailboat radioed: "Rapidly sinking -water up to knees in cabin - going over side in two dinghies." At 5.32 pm the Coast Guard received the last transmission, a child's voice counting as told so anyone listening could plot their position.

The distress calls were answered by several ships, including the U.S. Navy aircraft carrier *Roosevelt*. A search plane took off, but it was dark by then, and the crew landed at a nearby airfield rather than return to the carrier after a foray yielded no sign of the boat. The Coast Guard search of an 1,800-mile area was hampered by heavy seas and poor visibility. In spite of the fact that a person's chance of survival in seas outside of the warmer Gulf Stream was estimated to be no more than twenty minutes, the search went on for five days.

On January 18, the Coast Guard called me in Fort Lauderdale, Florida, where I was living at the time to advise me that the search had been officially called off. One of the hardest things I have ever had to do in my life was to call our mother in Paris to tell her that her only son had been lost at sea. She died almost to the day one year later.

Tim Bowden, a distinguished foreign correspondent of the Australian Broadcasting Commission, eager for adventure, had crewed for my brother on the *Moonglow* in a voyage from Majorca to Barbados. In his book, "Spooling Through," about this and other adventures, he wrote of Chris: "Wherever the storm takes him, he goes as a guest."

In April 1964 issue of Motor Sailing magazine that featured Chris' article and photos of the *Moonglow*'s trip, the editor wrote: "Chris was a faithful lover of the seas and the winds that blow above them. He has returned to his true home."

Now a half-century later, my brother's words and his world come alive again in this chronicle of his voyage across the seas from Europe to America.

FOREWORD

Upon completion of my solitary eighty-four day transatlantic voyage in July 1959, I was urged by many friends to write my experiences in book form. Much as I was tempted to do it, I felt that a purely factual account of my voyage would not render faithfully the true value of my adventure. There is no doubt in my mind that my experience is of a definite value, although one cannot measure it in dollars and cents or any standards commonly applied nowadays to any form of productivity. The values I speak of are intangible and, most of the time, invisible to the majority of humans who, in their constant mad pursuit of material gains, have no desire nor time to stop long enough to take stock of their lives and try to understand the inborn urge for adventure in nearly every person. Fewer still are those who want to or can break away from the bonds which modern society imposes upon its members. I do not advocate for one moment that the prospective adventurer rebel or try to overthrow the existing laws or the established social order, customs and conventions.

The fulfillment of the urge for adventure is intimate and individual in form. Different people express it in different ways. Liberty of choice and freedom from adherence to a pattern are among its beauties. By adventure, I mean the inner longing to live an exciting experience. I would further qualify by adding that it ought to be a clean, moral and beautiful experience.

The creative urge invariably goes along with the wish for adventure. We like to see purpose in such undertakings, although I am inclined to argue that the satisfaction of the desire for adventure is a valid objective in itself.

I am not against the unusual in adventure making. I do not condemn such enterprises as Colin Mudie's attempt to fly the

Atlantic in a free balloon via the upper trade wind route or Dr. Hans Lindemann's two amazing crossings of the Atlantic in a dugout canoe and a kayak or Dr. Alain Bombard's spectacular drift from the Mediterranean to the Caribbean in a rubber raft. All had valid reasons for what they did, although perhaps the element of beauty was missing in all three instances. I mention these adventurers because I followed their fates closely and met two of them later.

Seafaring will, to my mind, forever remain the most classic form of adventuring. A long-distance voyage in one's own sailing vessel cannot be surpassed as the ultimate expression of what all who embrace adventure seek. It is the purest of all adventures.

For many years before my voyage, I lived vicariously through the adventures of other men, and I was grateful they cared to put on record their experiences for others to share. At the time of my arrival in New York after making my own solo voyage, I was not ready to evaluate my experience. I felt that my judgment might be distorted by many months of solitude at sea. Moreover, my immediate reaction after landing in New York was that of great emptiness and a sense of loss. I had lived so long with my dream, and suddenly it was gone. The dream had become a reality and, in turn, a thing past. I could no longer look forward to my adventure. I was too near it to look back. The sense of satisfaction and achievement was not strong enough to counterbalance the depression that overtook me. In such circumstances I was not able to write about the experience. But the idea of a book lived on in my mind. I needed the perspective of time. I contented myself with writing articles for several magazines. It was not until many months later, while fishing out of Gloucester, Massachusetts, in the fall and winter of '59 that I began to write. It was a cold and boring business, this fishing, so I took myself off to the Caribbean where I continued to write on and off, cruising on the one hundred nine-foot schooner *Le Voyageur*. Then I took the fifty-six-foot schooner *Oronsay* from Martinique to New York. My son, Mark, joined me as mate. He had grown enormously since our Mediterranean winter. *Ornosay* became the *Caroline*, and I brought her back to the Caribbean where finally I felt ready to put down my story.

This is not a day-by-day account of a voyage, nor is it a log or a travelogue. I give a considerable amount of detail about my boat, the conditions encountered and so on. But these serve as a background to thoughts on what I like to call the philosophy of adventure, the romance of the deep-sea voyage.

Each deep-water small boat sailor has his particular idea of the voyage he dreams about and prepares for. Some settle for nothing less than circumnavigation of the globe. They are the aristocrats of this strange breed who choose to roam the seas in small sailing crafts. Amongst those, the single-handlers are kings. So far, fewer than a dozen men have sailed around the world alone. The multiple difficulties of such a voyage are beyond the comprehension of people who live on land. The effort entailed is not just a short burst of energy followed by a rest. A round-the-world voyage takes years of effort and degrees of physical and mental assertion of which few people are capable.

Some feel the pull of islands or a particular sea like the Caribbean or South Pacific. Still others are challenged by the capes that seem to have been put there to be sailed around like the Cape of Good Hope, Cape Leeuwin or the famed Cape Horn. Some believe that a simple crossing of an ocean will satisfy their ambitions. I always belonged to this latter school of dreamers. From the time I was a boy growing up in Poland, I felt a strange fascination for the Atlantic. This was the nearest ocean, something tangible and within easy reach, or so I thought. There were the North Sea and the Baltic, and beyond that was the Atlantic. An empty ocean, yes, but to me the emptiness is more of an attraction than a hindrance. The Atlantic is also one of the best bodies of water to make the voyage I always dreamt of – a trade wind voyage. On the other side is America, an attractive goal and a good conclusion to a lonely passage of several months' duration.

Ever since I had my first contact with the sea, the Baltic of my childhood, and since I read my first account of a small boat voyage, Alain Gerbault's "In Quest of the Sun," the story of his Pacific trip, the idea of an Atlantic crossing lived in my mind. Seldom, if ever, is a small boat voyage the result of a sudden decision. I believe you have to be born with the desire. The impulse has to be in you. The love of boats is seldom acquired. It is an inborn feeling.

To travel in small boats you do not have to love the sea. "Love of the sea" is a term invented by landsmen, by people whose experience of the ocean is limited to an occasional view from the safety of shore. How can you love something as cruel as the sea? There is untold beauty and fascination in the power of the sea. But it is cruel. How can you love something which is so cruel, something you have to fight and which is set to destroy you in the moment of your weakness. How can you love a woman who although beautiful is cruel, selfish and impersonal? You are fascinated by her beauty, you desire her, but you cannot really love such a creature. The sea, too, fascinates you, you are drawn to it, you want to conquer it.

In "The Call of the Sea," Adrian Seligman wrote of the "sea who loves no one and is forever unloved, who respects neither person, nor aim, nor the hopes and fears of men." However, he goes on to say, "Once you have acknowledged the sea's mastery, been chastened, disciplined and learned to fear it in the fullest sense, then the ocean which covers five-sixths of the earth's surface may for you become a place of peace. The calm routine, the daily occupation – making sails or painting ship or waiting for the sun at noon to tell you your position – these are peaceful occupations." True words, the fullest meaning of which I understood only after my own small boat voyage across the vastness of the sea.

Yes, the sea may become a place of peace. To achieve this, however, you must possess this inexplicable sense of love for sailing ships. This is a real love. A human, warm feeling of love for a dearest friend, this love also contains a sense of responsibility and duty to your ship. You care for her, you look after her, and you do not spare any efforts in keeping her fit and seaworthy. You do it with deep conviction that she will reciprocate. You know she will look after you when the ultimate conditions arrive. She will go on fighting when you lie below exhausted and frightened. She will remain faithful. She will not desert you. She will go on and save your life.

This is especially true when you sail alone. There are just the two of you – the ship and yourself – a team dependent on each other, trustful, bound by a common goal, sharing the same fate. There is grace and strength in a small sea ship. She helps you to fight your enemy, the sea. Her seagoing qualities will be decisive when you meet the challenge.

My dream remained a dream for many years. But it was always there for me to think about, to plan, to hope. It was not until 1958, when I reached the age of thirty-seven, that the circumstances played my way, not without a certain amount of prompting on my part, and I was able to go about this exciting business of executing a lifelong ambition. I was by then an experienced traveler. The whole of Europe was a familiar scene to me. South and North America were no strangers. North Africa was a second home. I had also managed to accumulate a considerable knowledge of small boats, sailing whenever conditions permitted, reading all the time. These travels were, however, dictated by the necessities of life rather than the wish to visit foreign lands and people. I cannot remember having once traveled as a tourist. Thank heavens for that. There was adventure galore in those travels – narrow escapes, strandings, many a difficult moment. But my life's greatest adventure was yet to be lived. Sailing across an ocean in my own ship. This was adventure in its purest form, at last within my reach.

– Christopher de Grabowski,
   Virgin Islands, June 1961, on board the *Caroline*

CHAPTER ONE

The early afternoon was very still and desperately hot. The thin white haze in the sky seemed to double the strength of the nearly vertical sun, diffusing its blinding light onto the desolate landscape, blending into a monotonous yellowish shade the meager colors of the southern Tunisian desert. Even the rows of the endless date palms, covered by dust of many rainless months, could not enliven the inherent sadness of this land, unfit, it would seem, for any form of human or animal existence. The big square fortress like a house upon the hill, between the plantation and the desert to the north, seemed unreal under the blazing sun and yet a visible proof of man's determination to subsist. I turned and walked towards this graceless monument on the edge of the Sahara Desert.

The courtyard, enclosed from all sides, hit me like an open furnace as I went across to my quarters. It was cooler there, thank God. The two-foot-thick walls and the small, screened windows kept the temperature a decent level, ninety degrees; perhaps it was a hundred twenty outside. I slumped gratefully on the cot and closed my eyes.

It was the end of August, my third week in this God-forsaken place at the oasis of El Djemna. I was completing, or rather trying to complete, a documentary film for the United States Information Agency in Tunis. Everything seemed to have gone wrong since I'd taken the assignment many months before. The equipment took ages to arrive, the local authorities were not interested in giving their support, and it was one of the hottest summers on record. My health was breaking down. I had a violent attack of hay fever, a touch of dysentery and an infection in my nose. I was worried. It was important that I keep fit, for this was my last job for the Agency which I was leaving after more than five years. My only camera had broken down, and I had to send it with a car and driver to Tunis for repair.

I was alone in the big house, a place with six bedrooms and as many baths, with fixtures a quarter of a century old. It had been empty for many years. One room was used as an office by the Tunisian manager. The rest was falling into bits and pieces. Dust lay thick on the cracked furniture and piles of old books and magazines. The noble Frenchman, the founder of the place was long since dead. A vast collection of sun helmets and walking sticks in a closet in the master bedroom were the only signs of his past visits. There was a portrait of the Old Man in the sitting room, an imposing figure with a white beard, the Duke of Clermont-Tonnaire. It was rather good, I thought, both the name and the portrait.

I was lucky to be able to make this our headquarters, for there was nothing livable for miles around. There was water in the bathrooms, now and again, and one could even, with some luck, flush the toilet in the morning. The pantry sported an ancient kerosene refrigerator. It took about three days to make an ice cube, but it was quite exciting to watch the daily freezing process and anticipate the delightful cold drink one would have in a day or two.

The oasis of El Djemna, where filming was done, lay ten miles to the south. It was the last but one inhabited area in Tunisia. After that there was nothing more. I had come across the spot some time before, and for a long while it was my favorite oasis in the whole of North Africa. I would have liked to remember it as I saw it the first time.

Evening was falling, and a mild sandstorm was blowing. Sand dunes were forming across the dirt road. Progress was difficult. We swung off the beaten track toward the cluster of dwellings, slightly up the hill, and then quite suddenly out of place, it seemed, there was one of the most enchanting spots I ever saw. A large pool of water, black in the fading light, mysterious, cool, peaceful. Tall palms, incredibly graceful, leaned over their feet in the yellow sand, soft looking, inviting for a rest. Silent buildings up on a cliff dropped to the edge of water. All very quiet, sheltered, not a soul in sight. Romance, peace and security were in that bit of water. Soon all was darkness, and the spell was broken. We went back to the car and drove away to the accompaniment of the strengthening wind and the eerie tune of the moving sands.

How I hated the place now. Gone were the romance and peace. Under the brilliant light of day, the pool was dirty and full of insects. Clouds of flies, persistent and hungry, swarmed back and forth from stinking latrines. There was dust, penetrating, annoying dust. But above all, there was the heat. Excruciating, exhausting heat. You couldn't run away from it. It followed you everywhere, all the time, sapping your energy, dehydrating your body, drying out your brain.

There was one compensation – the people. I could not help feeling attracted to these people. Their poverty had to be seen to be believed, and yet there was dignity and pride in their bearing, and there was a feeling of security and peace in their humble life. They rushed nowhere, hoped for nothing in this life. Absent was the fear of losing time or material things, for how can you lose anything if you have nothing at all? Their lives were spent in hard toil on the verge of starvation, accepting cheerfully the will of Allah the Merciful, who surely would not deny them the delights of paradise as a reward for their patient resignation to the hardships of their existence on earth.

I lay on my cot meditating about the past, the present and the future, letting the afternoon drag on, hoping the heat would wear off and the evening bring some relief. It usually did. I was most anxious to bring the job to some conclusion. It was getting late in the year. There was not much time left if I wanted to carry out my plans with a reasonable expectation of success. I was giving up the job in Tunisia to make my home in the country which through my long association with the Agency I came to know and love. I respected and believed in the sound and humane principles on which the Americans had built their nation. Now life was giving me a chance to become part of this community. I was anxious to finish my job and be on my way, for the voyage ahead was long and not easy.

Some three hundred miles to the north, in the outer harbor of Tunis lay my ship, the *Tethys*. She was a splendid example of a small deep-seagoing vessel. She was there, partially fitted out, and I was most eager to join her to complete the many jobs before she could be pronounced read to fulfill my lifelong dream: a wind voyage across the Atlantic. She was going to be my means of transportation to America, my new home or, should I say, our new home, for my twelve-year-old son, Mark, was to sail with me. Marina, my wife, was to follow some time after by air. With Mark on board, I felt I had no right to take any chances. The ship had to be as perfect as I could make her. Basically she was well-suited for an ocean passage. Her hull was immensely strong (this saved our lives some three months later). She was short-ended, long-keeled and reasonably fast and steered herself easily. But she had no equipment. The sails and rigging were old. The accommodations had to be improved.

I knew her well, for she belonged for many years to a good friend, Bep Patti, who had her built by a local craftsman under his special supervision. Every bit of timber was carefully chosen and fitted. After ten years she was as good as new. It was shortly after my return to America that I learned that Bep had put her up for sale. I grabbed her at once. Bep was looking for a larger ship. I knew I could find no better.

The transfer of ownership was speedily performed by my friend Maitre Charles de Cuzy, a keen sailing man himself. Sometime before I had told him of my intention of settling in America, and when I came to sign the sale contract he guessed at once. "And you will go in the *Tethys*?" I said yes but bade him to keep the matter between ourselves.

So *Tethys* became mine in February. I at once began to prepare her for the voyage. My plans at the time were quite fluid. It was to be a single-handed affair. My immigration visa was still an unknown quantity, but I was so eager to make the voyage that I was scheming to obtain a long leave of absence from the U.S. Information Agency, make the voyage and then resume my duties. To use the favorite expression of the Information people, the whole thing had to be played by ear! It was difficult to keep to one single line of action. Plans had to be changed and adapted as I went along. In this game of long-distance voyaging in small boats, the important thing is to press on. Otherwise one simply does not get anywhere.

In April I was away on the east coast of Tunisia in the charming town of Sousse helping to prepare the USIA stand at the local fair when Marina telephoned me with the wonderful news that my immigration visa had come through. It was to be a one-way voyage then. Some weeks later I met Bep in one of the busy streets of Tunis. He knew my taste for deep water and was speculating as to where I was planning to voyage in *Tethys*. I had just come out of the office, it was late afternoon, and obviously time for refreshment, so we walked to the nearest bistro to exchange ideas. "Now tell me, what are you going to do with *Tethys*?" Bep fired the question point blank, unable to hold on any longer. "Why, I will sail her to America, of course," I said, trying to look very casual. He stared at me for a long while, emptied his glass in one go, looked some more and uttered. "But in that case I am coming with you!"

And so we became four: a twenty-five-foot sailing boat, two men and a boy of twelve, with our goal nearly six thousand miles away by the trade wind route. We talked for a long while that evening, planning, and discussing the various routes. Finally it was agreed that we should sail in early fall, try to reach Gibraltar by the quickest route, then start across in December via the Canary Islands, the West Indies, on to Florida and New York. Little did we know how very different the reality would be.

Everything ends eventually, and so did my stay in the south. Within a week I was back in Tunis, sick, tired and in need of a rest. Another six days went by before I was fit to go on board. I still worked in the office, but the summer schedule gave me all afternoons free, which I spent preparing for the shakedown cruise. It was already decided that Mark should sail with us. He was keen, excited and helped with various jobs.

I asked for a three-week leave. On a Sunday toward the end of September, Mark and I sailed for Malta, a round trip of some five-hundred miles. This was to test the equipment, and training for Mark. I also wanted to get paint, a manila rope and other items not available in Tunis. Bep was in Europe. He was to return sometime in October. By profession an agricultural engineer, Bep was running his family vineyards, a job which gave him a considerable amount of free time from October to March. He was to join us for final preparations. We were to sail by November 1.

The shakedown cruise lasted exactly three weeks and was successful in every aspect. We had all kinds of weather from flat calm to a gale. We were four days outward bound and ten coming back with a full week in Malta. Among the kind, round-faced people in Valetta, we were fortunate to meet Joe Bezzina, who provided all the items I wanted, and his workshops did several jobs. We took provisions, visited the town, walked, went to the pictures, bathed and relaxed. I was satisfied with the ship and my improvements to the gear. There was great excitement one morning when, on our way back, some ten miles from the Italian Island of Pantelleria, Mark found an abandoned rubber dinghy. It was a French naval fighter pilot's one-man dinghy. It must have been at least three months in the water, partially submerged but in very good condition. We fished it out and added it to the ship's equipment. Subsequently the French Embassy in Tunis made inquiries, but its origin was never traced in spite of the serial number.

Although I had lost considerable weight during the summer in the desert, I felt fit and strong. I was, however, a little worried about Mark. His general physical condition was superb, but he had developed a tendency to seasickness which, on previous shorter cruises in other yachts, was never apparent. He bore it extremely well and with great patience, but I had doubts as to whether he could stand the strain of a long voyage. I said nothing waiting for his reaction. He kept quiet, but I saw he felt uneasy.

It was three a.m., also a Sunday, when we picked up our mooring at the La Goulette Yacht Club in Tunisia. We had to row her in, for the wind fell flat. We were both tired after ten days at sea and slept late that morning. The day was brilliant, and by noon we had our ship clean, dry and in order.

We were below stowing our personal gear when I broached the subject we dared not discuss at sea. I said, "Mark, I want so much to have you with me, but I am very much afraid that you will suffer a lot because of your seasickness. I think that perhaps it would be better for you not to come."

He did not answer but turned away and started to pack his sea bag. I sat there not knowing what to say. I was so anxious to take him, and yet I knew the great responsibility of the decision. He was stuffing his yellow oilskin into the bag when he could hold it no longer. Tears streaming down his suntanned cheeks, he faced me and said, "Paps, I must come with you, please take me, I want to help you so much!"

I gave in at once, my heart full of pride and love for my son. I never regretted the decision. In the hard months that followed, Mark was a constant joy to the rest of the ship's company. His seasickness gradually faded away. He bore the hardships with cheer and patience. And when on several occasions the sea had reached its grandest mood and we were fighting for our lives, he showed a courage many grown men could envy. I was proud of this little chap. Proud of his courage, his persistence, his powers of resistance to danger and physical discomfort.

The die was cast. We were committed to go. From that moment on events moved fast. Two days later I wrote a letter of resignation. It was sad, for I was giving up what had become a way of life. I felt, however, that I had done my share of the job. It was time to move on, and as compensation there was a great adventure ahead. I had a fine little ship, a splendid crew and my goal was America, the greatest country in the world.

CHAPTER TWO

The following two weeks were hectic as any pre-departure time. I became nervous and rather unpleasant to those around me. Time was pressing, October was coming to an end, and I wanted to sail on November 5, my birthday. There were still dozens of jobs to be done: the ship had to go on the slip, the double staysail rig made, provisions stowed and the many personal belongings somehow fit below in a now very restricted space. Most importantly, the main hatch canvas hood was still to be made and installed. It would be finished the day before we sailed.

Meanwhile, we celebrated Mark's twelfth birthday. We gave him an eight-shot automatic sports rifle and five hundred rounds of ammunition. So now the ship was well armed. I also had to wind up my private affairs. Many people had come to know about our voyage, and there were constant questions as to when we would sail. Apparently all wanted to come see us off, so I was cautious not to disclose the day. Mark was busy on the many fathoms of wrinkles for the main shrouds. Bep took charge of the fresh provisions, medical chest and cooking equipment.

November 1 found us still on the slip but otherwise ready. We moved on board to get used to living in the tight space. The night before, we had dined at the home of David MacKillop, the American Charge d'Affaires, in the absence of Ambassador G. Lewis Jones, who was receiving George Allen, the director of the U.S. Information Agency. The place was crowded. Allen surrounded by a tight circle of people anxious to please, so I had no chance to listen to what the head of the Agency had to say. In any case, my mind was already elsewhere. This was the world I was leaving behind. There was really no use trying to hold on to it.

I have only a vague recollection of the days that followed. I did not keep a diary, and just a few things stand out in my mind. The rest of the picture is blurred and unclear as the weather at that time, which was rainy and blowy. Back at the mooring, we loaded nearly three hundred cans of provisions, a gift from Sylvia and Bob Blake of the American Embassy. I can also remember a visit of an elderly American lady who came to see the crazy people who were going to risk their lives in a small boat. She didn't have the foggiest idea what sailing was about but would not have missed the sight, just in case. What a difference a visit of two friends made. Edouard Lahamy and Jimmy Tambone came to wish us bon voyage one morning bearing as a parting present – a splendid tray of fine Tunisian workmanship.

Finally we were ready. I had told friends that we would sail at noon on Sunday, but I had a firm intention to be off early on Saturday. A little deceit, yes, but I just did not feel I could have stood up to all the good-byes and handshaking. I felt it would be difficult to face them again if anything went wrong. Five months later when I was leaving Tangier for America, alone, many people came to see me off, but then it was different. There was no likelihood of my coming back.

Day was breaking when I called my crew on deck that Saturday, November 8. It was cold. The wind was in the northwest, a headwind. Not the best of starts, I thought, but we were committed to sail. By seven-thirty, I had her swinging to the mooring, and we were setting sail. The club was deserted at this early hour, just as I wished it to be. I delayed a little, hoping my wife, Marina, would come. I was about to cast off when she arrived with two cameramen friends. She was wearing, I noticed, my favorite kilt and a navy jacket I liked so much. She stood there, a sad little girl, wishing Godspeed to her departing menfolk. I waved a last good-bye and looked back no more. *Tethys* was gathering speed. I ordered the jib to be set. Bep handed me the helm, and we stood out to sea.

We were two hours out and sailing fast with one reef in the main when Bep came on deck, a worried look on his face. "She leaks," he announced briefly and disappeared below, apparently for further investigation. I made no comment, awaiting a complete report, but it was hardly good news so early in the voyage. Meanwhile, I had also noticed that she behaved strangely. She heeled more than usual and felt sluggish. Obviously she was overloaded and her stability upset. At that I was not too surprised, for we had an enormous amount of gear on board. All seemed important when we prepared the lists, but now it was equally important to take off some of the weight. Mentally I began to review the equipment, calculating how it could be reduced and the best way to dispose of it.

We had a total of fourteen sails on board. We bent on a brand new English suit and decided the old one, kept as a reserve, would have to go. There were three anchors. I thought two would suffice, but Bep had arrived the night before we sailed with a third one in hand, more cable and chain. Secured on deck also were: a sea anchor, two sweeps, two boathooks, two spinnaker booms for the twin staysails, mooring ropes, fenders, four cans of oil, six cans of kerosene, a ten-gallon water breaker, two life rings, a heaving line, three buckets, two bags with fishing tackle, the lead line and a deck brush.

Below two rubber dinghies, four life jackets and distress signals completed the life saving equipment. There were two bilge pumps, one on deck, one below. The navigational equipment was complete. We had two sextants, three wrist watches of which my Omega Seamaster was to be used as the chronometer, a cabin clock with built-in alarm, barometer, steering compass and binnacle with electric and oil light in it, a hand-bearing compass and a telltale compass. We had a Homer radio receiver and spare batteries (to this I added an RDF aerial in the Balearic Islands). We had a complete set of English and French charts, pilot charts and sailing directions, lists of lights, H.O. 214 tables, air almanac (in Gibraltar I switched to Brown's Almanac), parallel rulers, dividers, pencils, slide rule, protractor, binoculars, Excelsior log with spare rotator, eight flashlights, fifty spare batteries and flags.

There were snare halyards and sheets (in fact, there was enough rope to replace all running rigging twice), sail covers and a sun awning, a bag with sailmaker's equipment, a complete set of tools, an axe, half a dozen knives placed handy all over the ship, odd pieces of wood for repair, paint, brushes and a bosun's chair.

In the galley there was a primus pressure stove and a spare one in the after locker, a complete set of cooking pots and pans, crockery and cutlery, cups and glasses, and a large thermos flask. Each member of the crew had four blankets, sheets, a suit of oil skins and sea boots, four sweaters and a bagful of other clothing. Mark embarked with two enormous bags containing his most treasured possessions, among which were a baseball bat, two gloves, a collection of comic books, a tropical helmet, swimming goggles and flippers, an air gun and his sports rifle. I had twenty of my favorite books, a couple of sailing trophies and a bag with photographic equipment. Bep bought along a duplicated set of sailing directions in French, a portable radio set, two cameras, ten gallons of his excellent wine and a djellaba, a long hooded Moroccan robe.

The catering department was well stocked: three hundred cans of food, a variety of fresh provisions, fifty gallons of water, two cases of Scotch and half a dozen bottles of rum. The last two items were of greatest convenience during extreme weather conditions we were to meet later. There was, of course, a complete medical chest. The cabin was lit by a kerosene lamp in gimbals for which we had a dozen spare glasses. In addition there were electric reading lights over each bunk. It was a miracle that we managed to fit everything in. After all, the boat was only twenty-five feet on deck with a displacement of less than four tons, and we were three on board.

All that first day we spent beating north out of the Gulf of Tunis. The excellent Whale bilge pump was well able to cope with the leak, which, Bep discovered, was in the stern just above the water line. As she floated below her normal marks, this combined with rather hard going made water. I consulted Bep and Mark, and we decided to put into Bizerta, a fine harbor on the northern coast of Tunisia.

*****

The first few days out in a small boat are never comfortable. Forty-eight hours of beating was all we could stand up to. There was torrential rain, and the first night we spent hove to under close-reefed canvas in the lee of Cape Farina. Monday morning saw us entering Bizerta. It was very cold but clear as we tacked in the smooth waters of the outer harbor. There was work to be done. I was eager to press on. I wanted to sail as soon as we had coped with the leak and had unloaded the stuff I thought we could do without. The only damage suffered on that short passage was the broken binnacle glass when Mark sat on it while fooling in the cockpit with Bep. How very destructive a small boy's bottom can be, I thought with amazement.

We beat for a full two days and sailed over a hundred miles to make good sixty to land, still within an hour's drive of Tunis. But this was only a small sample of things to come.

Within an hour of landing, after a hearty breakfast, we went to work. The locker under the cockpit had to be emptied to get down to the leak. Bep dealt with it in a most efficient manner, and it was calked without the necessity of going on the slip. Meanwhile, I had selected items which had to be left behind. All in all we lightened the ship by some five hundred pounds. The water breaker went as did the old suite of sails, the third anchor, mooring ropes, two cans of oil, the pressure cooker and fifty fathoms of old rope. I had also asked the crew to comb through their personal effects and discard all superfluous items. Mark parted with his air gun, baseball bat and fifty pounds of comics.

I unloaded all the books, keeping only a few reference works amongst which Humphrey Barton's "Atlantic Adventurers," Garret Smith's "Arts of a Sailor" and an autographed biography of Habib Bourguiba, the president of Tunisia. I also kept a small atlas and my favorite book on underwater exploration by Hans Haas. Bep left his sextant, some clothing and all his French sailing directions.

By the end of the day, we were ready, but the northwesterly blow of great violence which had meanwhile developed kept us a full four days in port. I paid a visit to the governor of the province who was already aware of our voyage. I also talked on the telephone with Marina. She did not want to come; it would be too unsettling to go again through all the good-byes.

It was raining most of the time we were there, which did not prevent Mark and Bep from spending the mornings fishing and the afternoons in town. I preferred the comfort of the cabin. I would have enough soaking at sea, I thought. I spent many hours poring over the charts trying to find the best and safest way of getting to Gibraltar. There were two choices. One was to follow the North African coast at a distance of thirty miles, the other to go northwest toward the Balearics and then southwest. The first route was shorter, but there were strong easterly currents, and it was less safe in case of a northwesterly gale which could pin us to the coast where shelter was not easy to find. Bep was in favor of following the coast, and finally I decided to risk it. It nearly ended in a disaster.

On the coast of Algeria, the sea was running high. Wind came in gusts from the northwest. The torrential rain beat noisily on the canvas cockpit hood under which I was seeking shelter while surveying the dismal scene around me. How thankful I was for this hood put on the day before our departure from Tunis. There was nothing more I could do on deck. We were lying-a-hull ten miles north of Cape Carbone on the coast of Algeria.

I slid down the companion, not an easy thing in my heavy foul weather rig. I sat on the binnacle to get hold of the steel hood frame above my head, swung my legs inside, and I was in. The cabin was warm and cozy. It was hard to believe a gale was raging outside. Mark was in his bunk listening to a program from France on the ship's Homer receiver. Bep was asleep in the starboard berth. I took off my dripping coat and lay down on the cabin sole. It was better than trying to wriggle into the bunk under the low foredeck. The cabin clock, I noted, stood at ten minutes past midday. The date was November 21. We were fourteen days out of Tunis.

Mark turned around and peeped over the high canvas guard. He smiled at me and said, "You look tired. Rest now and don't worry. It will pass." How grateful I was for this encouragement. I patted his blond head and assured him that I wasn't worried in the least, but my heart was heavy with anxiety for the safety of the ship and my crew. We were in the shipping lane, visibility was nil, and each gust of wind was setting us close to the lee shore. Mark's supreme confidence in the boat and my seamanship made me so much more aware of the responsibility I had taken upon myself. I felt I could under no circumstances let my crew down. Mark had entrusted his young life in my hands, and I was going to do my best to bring the ship safely to her destination.

I was bothered by the terribly slow progress we were making. In two weeks, all I could show was one hundred fifty miles made good. And now we were being set back from whence we came. I no longer had illusions as to the length of our Mediterranean passage. It would be very long, but never did I suspect that three and half months would to go by before I would reach Gibraltar, alone!

We remained hove to under bare pole the rest of the day and the following night. Most of the time we slept. It was the first serious storm of the voyage, and we were not yet properly acclimatized. Appetites were poor, but I tried to keep us fit by cans of fruit, hot cocoa and biscuits. Bep and I were making frequent visits on deck to look for ships. I let Mark sleep in my bunk. There was no point in disturbing him.

Towards two a.m. the gale tapered off. The periods between squalls became longer, and the sea ceased to break. We were also out of the shipping lane, for I saw two ships pass miles to the north. The visibility had improved. A weak moon was in the sky. We all slept soundly till dawn with our minds at ease, which only a successful weathering of a gale can give.

It was full daylight when I came on deck. The sea was still high, but there was no danger in it. Cape Bougaroni on the Algerian coast was to the southeast distant some six miles. There was a steamer heading west. I set a small jib and let her run before the wind now a mere force six. Bep joined me in the cockpit, and we sat in silence for a while. I was not sure of my next move. I wanted to keep at sea, but with the falling wind and a rough sea there was no chance to beat to the westward. I was equally unwilling to go into port. At least I did not want to be the first to surrender.

I was, therefore, most relieved when Bep made the suggestion. "Look here," he said, "we are all tired. Conditions are unfavorable. Why don't we head for a day or two into Collo? It's just eight miles beyond the Cape. We shall be there at noon."

I was still undecided. Mark came on deck and I asked his opinion. "It's all the same to me. I don't mind staying at sea, but you are the captain. Do as you think best," he said. The best, of course, was to go into harbor and wait. This way we could rest properly, dry out the ship, sleep and eat. Furthermore, we would not lose any more ground. In the position we were in, we would just drift to the east, without wind, and that always drives me mad.

"All right, we shall go in. Set the jib and staysail," I said, my decision made.

It was midafternoon when we entered the little harbor of Collo with hardly a steerage way on the ship. A motor launch full of French soldiers was going out. They waved and laughed. "Fancy you coming in here," one of them shouted. "A lousy place, this." But were thankful to be safely in, no matter how lousy the town.

By the time we had her tied up stern to the muddy quay and an anchor out, as is the fashion in most ports of the Mediterranean, an official-looking personage was waiting to greet us. There was a small crowd of soldiers looking with interest at the pleasure yacht, so very much out of place in this war-torn country.

As I climbed the high jetty, ship papers in hand, my eyes fell upon a pair of beautiful carpet slippers. I looked up curious to identify their owner. They belonged to a man of pleasant appearance dressed in a blue cloth working suit, a naval cap on his head. He introduced himself as the harbor master and invited us to proceed to his office where we could deal with all the formalities of entering the harbor.

He led the way through the small but crowded port area, zigzagging towards the entrance guarded by armed sentries. In the middle of the yard there was, I noticed, a watchtower complete with a machine gun and searchlights. There was barbed wire all around, and the whole place was alive with soldiers coming and going, armed and in field attire. Trucks were constantly coming in to pick up stores and war materiel. After a couple of weeks at sea it was strange, to say the least, to be in this atmosphere that breathed war at every step. We walked up the hill while I engaged my companion in polite conversation. Later that day, we heard gunfire in the distance. Mark was excited at being so close to a real war while to me it brought memories of my Second World War years.

We walked up the hill, and while I was giving a brief account of our voyage, I felt unable to take my eyes of his marvelous footwear. Coincidence, perhaps, but exactly one month later in the Spanish Island of Minorca, at Fornells, we were met by the harbor master dressed in a similar pair of bedroom slippers. A communion of thought of people following the same calling I suppose.

The harbor master was kindly disposed toward visiting ships. He felt we meant no harm, and the formalities were few. However, he said it was necessary due to the rather unusual circumstance, meaning the conflict, to obtain a landing permit from the representative of the French Navy. "Then," I said, "let's go and see him at once." He looked at me for a long while, then announced with dignity: "Monsieur, I am the representative of La Marine Nationale."

I made a feeble attempt to cover my gaffe, but the kind man dismissed the matter with a wave of his hand and gave permission to land without any further questions. I felt a deep sympathy for this Algerian Moslem, a French citizen who tried to do his duty and serve what he thought to be his country while another group of his kinsmen were fighting to create an independent Algeria. People like him were bound to suffer no matter how the conflict would end. There would be no place for him in the independent Algeria, and he could never truly hope to be fully assimilated into the French society. There was a melancholy look in his eyes when later, over a glass of beer, we talked of our voyage. I could feel he envied the freedom that was ours. There was no malice in it, just a resignation to an unavoidable fate.

We did not lose any time in going ashore. It was a poor place and had little to offer. The scene was a usual mixture of Europe and Africa. The setting was beautiful, a hilly peninsula, woods and beaches, a nice spot for a summer vacation – in peacetime. Now it was a base of operation against the Algerian forces. Fighting was not far off. That night we heard gunfire again. I felt sorry for both sides engaged in this draining struggle now in its fifth year.

The coastal roads were closed to traffic. All supplies were being brought by sea from the large port of Philippeville thirty miles to the east. In twenty-four hours, I noticed four small coasters coming in loaded to capacity with goods ranging from furniture and car tires to food and Champagne. Someone, as always is the case, was making heaps of money out of the suffering of others.

We turned in early that night. I wanted to take full advantage of our stay in port to rest properly. Moreover, toward nightfall a military Jeep stopped near the boat, and we were informed by a dashing captain of the French Army that there was a curfew in town and that we were liable to be shot without warning if we ventured into town after dark.

When cruising, the first night in port is always the best. You have either made a good passage and you are pleased with your performance or you are in after having gone through bad weather and you are glad to be in safely with the delightful prospect of a full night's sleep ahead. So this one was no exception. We ate on board, and there was much laughing and joking. I was watching with pleasure how well Bep and Mark were getting along. A bond of friendship was forming between them in spite of the difference in age. Bep with his cheerful disposition and great patience was an ideal companion for Mark, while his sea experience made him invaluable as a mate.

I fear I was the least jolly of our little ship's company. My mind was constantly occupied with many problems of the voyage, and my temper was short more often than I would have wished. I wanted to press on all the time. I was terribly eager to get into the Atlantic. I had calculated on a twenty-day passage to Gibraltar, well, thirty days at most, and we were fifteen days out with only one fifth of the seven hundred fifty miles done. The weather was the worst of any November I could remember for many years past. My morale was low, but I tried to look as cheerful as I could so as not to discourage Mark who never failed to give me encouragement and never complained. One day when we were becalmed in a confused and unpleasant sea, I shouted in utter desperation, my patience nearly exhausted, "How I wish we could be on the other side already!" Mark looked at me with a smile and quietly observed, "But then the voyage would be over, and you would have nothing to look forward to."

I remembered his words when in New York I was leaving my ship. Eight months and six thousand miles lay astern of me. Gales and calm companionship of my crew and the incredible loneliness of the long Atlantic voyage, adventure, romance of a deep-sea passage, the preparations, months of planning and final success – all that was already the past. I felt a great emptiness in my heart. Really, in that moment, I had nothing to look forward to. To travel hopefully is better than to arrive, a weather-beaten cliché perhaps, but how true.

I could not sleep that first night in port even though I was dead tired. I tuned the radio in my bunk to an all-night station in Paris and lay there listening to the music thinking how difficult it was to sail a twenty-five-foot sailing boat across the sea.

CHAPTER THREE

Next day, a Sunday, rose clear and sunny. We were all lazy and lingered in our bunks talking and urging each other to get up and prepare breakfast. Bep, the bravest of us all, as usual, took upon himself this important task and soon there was a sumptuous meal laid out on the piece of plywood we used as a table. There was fruit juice, eggs and bacon, porridge, fresh bread and butter and jam, and excellent coffee. While at sea Mark ate comparatively little, but in port his appetite was prodigious. He ate like a hungry young wolf. It was a pleasure to watch him stow away an amount of food which would suffice to feed two grown men. A sign of good health this, and indeed we kept marvelously healthy under these hard conditions. There was not as much as a sneeze on board. We did not put any fat on. In fact, we were all losing weight, but it did us no harm. The best proof was that in the three months that Mark was on board he grew nearly two inches, and later ashore he put on seven pounds in less than a month.

On board a sailing vessel, even a small one, there is always work to be done. Sails have to be dried, rigging checked, provisions re-stowed and, of course, there are the usual housekeeping chores rather awkward to perform because of the constricted space. After breakfast we threw all we could on deck, and we festooned the rigging with sails, blankets, oilskins, sweaters and other garments. She looked like a floating laundry shop.

After church, which was surprisingly well attended by the Army, including a general and his staff, Mark and I went in search of a restaurant while Bep returned on board. There was not much choice in the way of places to eat, but we were not fussy. I confess I prefer to eat out anywhere rather than cook.

The place we went to was very small and very crowded with soldiers. Old bemedaled campaigners mingled with young boys fresh out of training camp. All bore sidearms, all drank and laughed, trying to get as much amusement as they could out of this dreary little town and also, I suppose, trying to forget that only a few miles away, in the hills, lay mortal danger which soon they would be called upon to face. On the wall I noticed a sign which said: "All political discussion is forbidden." As far as I could make out, no one was eager to engage in such talk.

One of the major problems on board a small yacht, especially in winter, is washing. It is not easy to keep clean when it's cold, the weather stormy and the boat's washing facilities consist of a small basin. Moreover, water is a rare commodity not to be squandered. When coming into port, a small boat sailor wants, above all, a hot shower. I know of nothing more relaxing. The delight of stepping under streams of hot water after a sojourn aboard is unique. I know of no sensation as keen as that first contact with fresh water after days or weeks of confinement in layers of heavy winter clothing. You feel free, easy and clean. You soap yourself and wash away the dirt, then you soap yourself again and then some more. You let the health-giving liquid massage your tired muscles. Your mind becomes clear, fatigue vanishes, optimism returns. There is new strength in your body, the hardships of the passage are forgotten, you are ready to face anything. You believe, nay, you know, everything will come out as you planned. You are a new man.

Bep and Mark had discovered the previous day an Arab bath where apparently hot water was plentiful. Mark led us through the complicated little streets, muddy, miserable. Left, right, right again, the street became narrow and without an issue. There was a public toilet on one side, completely open, and a door to the right, apparently the entrance to the bathhouse.

The inside was dark and humid. Vapor escaping from some inner chamber infused the hall that served as a combination of office and dressing room. Mark who had been there the previous day instructed me in the science of temperature and condensation. The walls were dripping wet. A raised platform covered with mats ran along the right side of the room, and this, Mark instructed, was the place to undress. We stripped and with towels round our middle stepped into wooden sandals. An attendant led us through a small corridor to where the bathing was done. There was a row of cubicles with a wooden door, crooked and black with age. The stone floor slabs were worn out by many generations of bathers. There were channels dug by the water from the constantly dripping taps. There were no overhead showers but rather low taps. It was not easy to wash bent in half. But what a delight nevertheless. Mark screamed with pleasure in his cubicle next to mine. He sang and splashed and shouted. I don't suppose the ancient establishment had ever had a customer like him. We left an hour later, cleaned and much refreshed, declining the invitation to rest on the mats in the outer chamber.

Next day we sailed full of hope not knowing that we would come as near a disaster as I would ever care to be.

It was a pleasant sunny day with light westerly wind and a calm sea. The barometer was a little lower than usual, but I saw no reason to delay our departure for such a trivial matter.

We could just lay a northerly course, which I found convenient, for I wanted to make some offing turning west. Progress was slow all that day and the following night. By midday next day, we had made twenty-five miles to the west and Cape Carbone bore southwest distant some fifteen miles. The wind fell, and so did the barometer. We simply could not sail past this confounded cape, which we had first sighted six days ago. It is a maddening sensation to feel completely powerless to weather a silly headland, which is there to mock you for days and sometimes weeks.

Something in the air made me feel that bad weather was likely to set in. I hoped it would not be another northwesterly, but when in midafternoon a heavy squall came from the west, I had no more doubts. We were in for another gale and a severe one at that. I could tell it by the swell, which was short and fast. There practically was no wind as yet, but it was only a question of an hour or so before it struck, so I did not delay to reef her right down. We close-reefed the mainsail and set the storm jib of only fifteen square feet. The canvas fore hatch cover was put on and all well secured on deck. We left the log line streamed, for it gave good indication of our drift.

Early November dusk was falling when the wind came. I was astounded at the violence with which it struck. There was a gust and then another, and then it just began to blow great guns. There was no question of sailing, so I hove her to, but made the fatal mistake of doing it on the inshore track. The wind was from the west, and I thought we would be drifting east. It was not so at all, as we were to discover twenty-four hours later. We stayed on deck for a long time observing with pleasure how well the little *Tethys* rode the nasty seas. Her motion was so easy, so graceful. There was no effort in her lifting up to the short seas, which already had begun to break. The sails were setting perfectly. I never tired of looking at the beautiful curve of the mainsail, which even close-reefed had a perfect shape.

That evening, and right through the night, the wind increased in strength and veered to the Northwest. By midnight it was a full gale and by no means at its peak yet. Bep and I were making frequent visits on deck to watch for commercial shipping. Visibility deteriorated hour to hour. There were low clouds, and the night was terribly dark. The coast, still visible late in the afternoon, had disappeared. I no longer had any means to check our position and had to rely entirely on my good judgment of the drift. At that time I had no radio direction finder on board, a grave oversight, not having that RDF.

Mark was comfortably tucked away in my bunk under a pile of blankets. By that time he had developed such confidence in the ship, her captain and her mate that he thought nothing at all of the storm. From time to time he inquired how she was riding, what the position was and whether there were any ships in sight. He heard me ask for that information often in the past, so naturally he was now forming a habit of watching these important details himself. It was clear he felt secure and relaxed. There was a funny program from France on the radio. He had magazines and comics all around him and an open can of chocolate biscuits into which he was digging with astonishing regularity.

Bep and I felt less cheerful. I had kept my sea clothing and safety belt on. I found it too tiring to undress each time I came below so I just relaxed between the bunks on the cabin sole fully dressed, ready to jump on deck at any moment.

Toward dawn it began to rain heavily. I was surprised that the wind, instead of tapering off, actually increased. It was now blowing a good sixty knots, and it was time to take the mainsail off. I had the impression that the rain would have a moderating effect on the wind. The torrential downpour kept the sea down, but the wind came stronger every minute. It was now a strong gale.

Bep, always an early riser, was up at the crack of dawn and spent all morning peeping through the main hatch, watching the sails, the sea, the rain. I, as usual, found it more comfortable to lie between the bunks with all kinds of cushions wedged around me. In any case, there was nothing to be seen outside, for the visibility was reduced to not more than a few yards. I had, in fact, never experienced such thick weather in the Mediterranean. By nine a.m. it was gusting seventy knots. It was clear that we would have to strip her of all canvas.

After one particularly violent and prolonged gust, Bep suggested we take down all sail. It's strange how one's mind works in such conditions. As soon as the idea of danger penetrates your brain, you feel that action must be taken immediately, even if the conditions have been constant for the past half-hour and nothing has happened.

So I was on deck instantly. My heart nearly leaped up to my throat with fright when the full force of the wind hit me. I thought the mast and all the rigging would fly right out. It was difficult to stand upright on deck. The horizontally driven rain came in solid sheets, pouring into my sleeves and under my sou'wester. Bep took position by the halyards belayed to pins on the port pinrail, and I remained aft. When close-reefed, the mainsail boom touches the gallows, unless the topping lift is set to make it clear. So the first action is to ease off the lift, then sheet the boom right in on top of the gallows. The halyards are let go, and while one man forward pulls on the luff, the other controls the leech keeping the sail full of wind and under no circumstance allowing it to flap. Once down, a lashing, which is permanently attached to the gallows, is passed around the boom and gaff, and the sail is secured. Then three or four gaskets are put round the sail, the mainsheet is coiled and hung in its loops on the gallows, and the deck is clear. A simple maneuver, but it took us a full twenty minutes. Most of the time we were hove down on our beam ends with part of the coach roof under water. How small and defenseless our boat looked at the moment, and how I wished for more freeboard. To take in the jib was a simple matter.

With no sail, *Tethys* at once took a broadside position drifting to leeward at what I estimated a knot and a half. She rode nicely, so I thought it unnecessary to try the sea anchor. I was tired, and I wanted to avoid all the business of setting it. Actually I should have done so, for it would have reduced the drift to less than a knot. I thought vaguely of the easterly current, which must have increased considerably, but my mind's danger alarm still did not ring, and I took no action. In fact, there was no action I could have taken except, perhaps, to stream the sea anchor.

The wind was now in the northwest and gusting eight knots and more. At about two p.m. the rain moderated, and the sea started building up to an alarming size. We were broadside on and safe. The rather fast square drift made it smooth to windward, and the breaking crest would collapse before reaching us. The boat was immensely strong and could stand a lot of beating. I had no qualms on that account. What really worried me was the lee shore drawing nearer each hour. Real danger hid in the low-lying clouds. I was not sure how far we had drifted, and I was anxiously peering to the southeast for any signs of land. My friend Boris Lauer-Leonardi, the editor of The Rudder, had once written to me: "The sea will not harm you. It is the land you should beware of." How right he was. I always had a particular dislike of sailing near the coasts. To me, yachting is sailing from port to port across the sea, not following the coast. It really is voyaging more than pure sailing. I don't mind staying at sea for long periods. A good boat can weather a severe storm safely, providing there is sea room. A lee shore is mortal danger. Few sailing yachts are capable of working off a coast in heavy seas and wind.

The afternoon dragged on without any apparent easing of the wild gale. The seas were dangerous, and little *Tethys* found it increasingly difficult to lift up to the steep breaking waves. The broadside on position was no longer safe, but I could not decide what to do next. Bep was fascinated by the wild conditions. He declared never having seen the blue Mediterranean in such tremendous fury. I fully shared his view. We both remained in the cockpit, frightened, tired and cold. Earlier in the day I had broken out a bottle of whisky, and now we tried to keep the weather out by frequent and generous swigs of this courage-giving liquid.

It was late afternoon when the clouds lifted and I saw land. I nearly panicked. Cape Bougeroni was just under our lee, not more than six miles distant. I began to take bearings, and in half an hour I knew that we could never weather it. The cape bore due east, and the bearings were diminishing in a slow but deadly shift, for the northwesterly was setting us on it directly. There was still time, I thought, to try to run past it steering eighty degrees. I put her on that course, and she ran at better than five knots under bare pole. The sea was enormous, breaking heavily on the port quarter, which meant I had to bear away toward the cape to meet the more vicious breakers exactly stern on. Bep kept a lookout to warn me of the approaching big ones.

We ran for our lives, praying for the wind and sea to calm down even if just a little. It was a terribly delicate and exhausting

27

business to keep her going that way, for the seas were very short. Ten minutes went by, and since I failed to correct her course, a big breaker came over the port quarter. It was a warning, but I ran on. Then I heard Bep shout as he ducked to take cover behind the stern dodge. I pushed the tiller to port with all my strength, but she did not answer. I felt her sluggish in my hand as she heeled over to starboard, water pouring over the port side. She began to ride sideways, her deck awash from stern to stem as she broached to starboard. For a moment, it flashed through my mind she might go right under. With her low freeboard, there was little reserve buoyancy to keep her floating under the tons of water. Cold sweat broke out all over my body. My heart stopped beating when I thought of Mark below. She rode thus for what seemed to me an eternity. All I could do was to hang onto the lifeless tiller and pray. The great sea hissed and foamed as *Tethys* lost her speed and stood up again. The immediate danger was past.

Bep and I sat in the cockpit weak with fright, trying to recover our calmness before either of us spoke. I slid the hatch open and shouted to Mark, "Are you all right?" His voice came back cheerful, "Why, yes, is anything the matter?" He never knew of the danger we experienced.

As always after a particularly big sea, there was a moment of peace, so we hurriedly conferred on the next step. Obviously there was no question of running under these conditions. We agreed that it was time to stream the sea anchor and somehow try to sneak past the fatal cape. We remained hove to while preparing the anchor which was secured on the cabin top. It was a simple operation to stream over the stern. In less then ten minutes I put her before the wind once more. I also asked Bep to hang one of the oil cans over the side to see what effect it would have on the breaking seas. I had never had the occasion to use oil before, so I was curious how it would work. The effect was quite astonishing. After a while there was a large and smooth patch, but as I kept the sea on the port quarter, it was not directly to windward. Our speed was then well under two knots, quite safe, but we began again to drift toward the cape.

All went well for a while when suddenly I felt the ship jump ahead and gather speed. "The anchor is gone," I shouted to Bep, and I hove to at once. "Get a second warp from below and some old sails," I called. Bep disappeared below with lightning quickness. He is superb on deck in hard conditions, so in a short while the improvised sea anchor went over the stern. The warp was a new two-inch manila, fifty fathoms long. The rope held us better than the sea anchor could ever had done. We slowed down appreciably. But the lee shore was now not more than three miles distant. I felt in the pit of my stomach the fear of what might happen if the gale did not ease up. Every few minutes I took a bearing with the hand-bearing compass. The bearings continued to decrease, which meant that we were being set toward the shore. It became clear that we could never weather the cape this way. The only escape was to make sail and try to get off.

It was risky, for the wind was gusting eighty knots, and the close-reefed main, although very small in area, was still too big. I feared we might lose the sail or even be dismasted. There was a trysail below, but I would not have the job of setting it. That would be too much under those conditions. I consulted Bep, and he agreed that we must set sail at once. I hove to once more, in came the fifty-fathom warp, up went the close-reefed mainsail and the storm jib, and the wild beat began.

Meanwhile, the wind had backed to the west-northwest, so I was able to lay a course slightly east of north with the wind abeam. But with the seas were still coming somewhat forward of the beam, I had to ease off the mainsheet. Even so, the boat was overpowered and would lie helpless, pinned down by the savage gusts, unable to make any headway. When I judged it was safe to do so, I would bear away a little and let her pick up the pace. Seas were now coming on board over the weather side, breaking with great violence on the exposed topsides and spilling right into the mainsail with such force that I thought the sails would split at any moment. I was tense, my mind on the job. Bep, sheltered under the cockpit hood, was ready for action.

Night had fallen. Cape Bougeroni light began to send its signals. Once more I took out the hand-bearing compass to fix our position. What a relief – the light bore three hundred five degrees – we were making headway! We were still drifting to leeward but were clearly getting away from the coast. Hours went by, dark, wet, anxious hours. The gear held. The ship stood up bravely to the horrible beating. I felt a great weariness come over me. We fought fatigue with whisky and lumps of sugar, both in liberal quantities.

By ten that night we had worked a fair distance off the cape, and I was beginning to relax when Bep, who was on the lookout for shipping as we were in the track of steamers by then, shouted a warning that a ship was coming at us from the west and was less than a mile off. I was of two minds: show some lights or keep her dark. Finally I decided to light the sails and let the steamer know our position. She kept on coming at us, so I kept on flashing a powerful light. She had the sea astern and could not keep a straight course. She swung a good twenty degrees to both sides of her course and would point as if to pass astern of us, then swing and point ahead of us. Indeed a dangerous situation, for I did not know whether to keep going, heave to, or jibe and run south.

When she was not more than a cable off, I switched the light out and put her before the wind. The steamer kept coming at us. I maintained speed so that I could detour at the last moment if she did not alter course. She was not more than half a cable when she began to turn to port. I knew then that she had seen us and was trying to investigate whether we needed assistance. We were in her lee by then and becalmed. I called Mark to come on deck and see the sight of this big steamer rolling in the seas. Mark sprang out, placed his head over the hood and caught a mighty blow from the swinging boom. He sunk back into the cabin with a moan, but promptly came on deck again grinning. "I'm not hurt, I'm not hurt," he shouted. Bep and I were making frantic signs for the steamer to go away, signaling that we didn't need anything and that she was a menace. She understood and drew away. We were alone once more. The sea is only a mild danger compared with a lee shore or steamers.

We continued north-northeast for another hour until I judged us to be ten miles off the cape bearing one hundred fifty degrees. We handed in the mainsail, and what a relief it was to let her forge ahead under the little storm jib only. There was no need for us to remain on deck any longer, so we scrambled below to rest. If the gale eased off, we would try to make Collo the next day. I got in my usual place between the bunks and fell asleep at once.

I woke up hours later. It was still dark. There was less wind. Bep was standing in the companionway. I called softly to ask what he thought of the weather. "The worst is past" was his hopeful answer. "Well, then, come on, go back to sleep," I said, for I felt he was about to suggest that we should start sailing. I for one had no intention of moving.

The morning rose bleak, wet and gray. There was a fair sea running, and *Tethys*, with only the little storm jib set, rolled. I lay for a long while trying to raise enough optimism to face another day. During the night we had made a considerable distance to the north. The coast to the south was a goodly eighteen miles away, or perhaps more. The visibility was none too good, so I could not identify any landmarks to take a fix. I knew more or less where Collo was. After a quick breakfast, we set a close-reefed main and started on our way.

All that day we made slow progress toward the coast. The wind had gone to the west and then began to head us. By evening we were in the lee of Collo, and it became a beat. The easterly current now very strong was setting us to leeward. The choppy sea made progress extremely slow and unpleasant. We had shaken our all reefs, but the violent gusts soon forced us top reef on, for at times she was overpowered. We made long tacks, gaining little each time. The water around us was brownish-yellow with tons of clay washed from the hills by the torrential rains of the past thirty hours.

It was a picture of desolation, and our nerves were on edge.

All we now wanted was shelter and a quiet night. It was dark when we came around the short breakwater to carefully make our way in. Bep was at the helm. I stood by forward ready to let go the Danforth anchor while Mark illuminated the sails with the big flashlight. I had no intention of becoming a target for some trigger-happy soldier. Down went the Danforth, we rounded up smartly, and Bep jumped ashore with the mooring ropes. Within ten minutes we were secured and the sails stowed neatly. No one came on board that evening, so by nine p.m. the ship's company was in profound sleep, resting after the ordeal of the storm.

From force of habit, I kept waking up every few hours. It rained heavily all night, but it was delightful to be in port. It was less pleasant, however, to think that we had now been nineteen days out of Tunis and had made good only one hundred fifty miles with still six hundred miles to Gibraltar. Most definitely this small boat sailing was proving to be a tough game. Would I ever succeed to take my ship across the Atlantic? I was beginning to wonder. There would be ample time to worry next day, I thought as I sank back into the welcome oblivion of sleep.

Our second appearance in Collo created a mild commotion among the authorities. By midmorning, while we were having a cup of coffee, two police inspectors arrived on board to investigate. Apparently they thought it highly suspicious that a small sailing boat should be cruising in winter for pleasure. I must say that our visitors, a Frenchman and an Algerian, were most correct in their behavior and tried to perform their duty with tact and courtesy.

They started off with general talk about the weather, then gradually guided the conversation to the purpose of our voyage, the ship, her crew and her equipment. I took the hint and showed them around. I explained how the gear was stowed and where, what we carried to be comfortable on board, the navigational instruments, our charts and food. For a moment, one of them took the Homer radio receiver for a transmitter. It is small but beautifully designed and looks most impressive. It was not difficult, however, to demonstrate that it was only a receiving set. A joking reference was made to the probability of our having disembarked passengers somewhere on the coast. I laughed away such an idea. "Who," I exclaimed, "would have cared to come in such a small boat, except crazy sportsmen like ourselves!"

There was, however, one thing on board which might have caused trouble, and that was Mark's automatic sports rifle and the considerable stock of ammunition. I well remembered the case of George Boston, an American from Swampscott, Massachusetts, on the north shore of Boston, who cruised these waters single-handed in 1954 in his thirty-foot Tahiti ketch, the *Fiddler's Green*. It was soon after the Algerian conflict began, so each vessel was rigorously inspected. He had two or three rifles on board and got into difficulty. Boston had been driven by bad weather to Philippeville, a large port thirty miles east of Collo. He was taken ashore and kept for three days under close observation before he could convince the authorities of his bona fide intentions. I was to meet him some years later at St. Croix in the Virgin Islands. He was on his schooner *Wander Lust,* and I on the *Caroline.*

With our Tunisian flag, we might have had considerable difficulty in proving our impartiality in regard to the Algerian situation. After all, Tunisia had strongly supported this war for independence. While in Tunis, I had never made a secret of my sympathy for the cause of independence. I was of two minds as to what to do. To say we had an arm on board or to keep quiet. Finally I decided to wait. If I were asked about arms, I would at once say yes. If not, I would just keep silent. After all, they were free to look everywhere and see for themselves. All went smoothly. After a while our visitors departed well satisfied that we had no evil intentions.

Three days later on December 1, we sailed for Palma de Majorca. All were in agreement to keep off this dangerous coast, and when, on the second day out, it faded in the distance, I was glad to see it disappear in the evening haze. Twenty-two days to make good one hundred fifty miles was more than we could stand. It was out third attempt to pass Cape Carbone. I hoped this time we would make it.

The distance between Collo and Palma de Majorca is just under 200 miles, not a great distance that, but after our experience off the Algerian coast, I was viewing this passage with some anxiety. I was, therefore, greatly relieved when, on the second day out, a smart northeasterly sprang up, and we were able to set a course directly for Cabrera Island on the southeastern tip of Majorca.

As usual with a northeasterly, it became cloudy, and the nights were dark, but we stormed along at a great pace, and my heart rejoiced. This was fine passage-making weather, and I was eager to make the most of the fair wind. We carried all sail. I stood watch with Bep. Mark sleeping all night, steered during daylight hours.

CHAPTER FOUR

What a wonderful feeling it is to see your ship press on, the log rotating merrily, each passing hour bringing you nearer to your destination. With a steady wind, life on board becomes regular and pleasant. Meals are properly cooked and eaten at ease, and there is ample occasion for housekeeping chores and rest. On the third day we sighted a family of whales. How exciting! They blew a mile or so away to leeward, but I was unwilling to go off the course to look at them. That same afternoon we spotted turtles. Mark spent an hour with his gun trying to get one for dinner in vain. I have never heard of any yacht being successful in catching a turtle.

That night we were but seventy miles off Majorca. When I came on deck at two a.m., the loom of Cabrera light was on the horizon dead on our course. We had taken two reefs earlier in the day. Now with the wind in the east and very strong, we made good progress. A running ship is a joy to handle, especially a ship like *Tethys* which seems to have been built for just that. She is safe and easy on the helm and holds her course well.

The approach of a strange coast at dawn is one of the delights of passage making, especially if it is an island. Although it is pleasant to sail near an interesting coast, I dislike long coastal passages. I always have the feeling that the same could be done in a car or train. An island, on the other hand, can only be reached by sea or by air. There is the satisfaction of achievement, and the sight of land is welcome after many days at sea. When coasting you can become tired of the slow moving landscape. I, for one, am always aware of the many dangers of the shore to a small sailing vessel without power. Humphrey Barton, who wrote about his own travels in "Atlantic Adventures: Voyages in a Small Craft," seems to be of just the opposite opinion. He likes coasting, but even he could not resist the lure of a deep-sea passage. He took his twenty-five-foot *Vertue XXXV* across the Atlantic from Lymington, England, to New York in 1950, he said, to sell her for dollars and aid the British export drive. But I am sure this was just an excuse for a voyage he wanted to make for its own sake.

It was a gray and overcast morning this December 4, but I felt elated and well pleased with the passage. The wind was force six, and I was making well over five knots. I passed to the south of Cabrera Island, an uninviting rocky group of small islands under the control of the Spanish Navy. There was a safe anchorage on one of them which could be visited by special permission of the navy. But now we were bound for Palma and Gibraltar. An extensive visit to the many bays and anchorages in the Balearics would have to wait until another time.

Bep and Mark came on deck as I was bringing her under the lee of land. We shook out all reefs and sailed at a great pace in the smooth waters. Up went all flags. She looked impressive with the Tunisian red star and crescent at the flag staff, the Slocum Sailing Club at the masthead, Spanish ensign on the starboard crosstrees and my vice commodore's pennant on port.

An ancient Spanish warship, a large minesweeper, was making for us. She came quite near flashing a message in Morse at very slow speed which, I confess with shame, I was unable to read. We waved in reply, and she made off. We sailed on straight for the harbor entrance. Bep had been here before in *Tethys* and was able to identify the entrance at a distance. Two pairs of small ships were sweeping in a channel marked with red and yellow flags. A fifth small unit came dashing at us, and we were ordered to get the hell out of the channel. We did so promptly.

A smart ketch was coming out of the harbor, so we went on to meet her. She was the first yacht we had seen on the voyage. We would not have missed the chance to look at her. She was an extremely attractive little deep-sea ship, Marconi ketch rigged with a stern cabin and a transom stern. She must have been at least thirty-six feet on deck. The wind was strong, she was under full sail, and so were we. We at once began to race with her, and so left her standing. A nice little ship, the only thing wrong was that she just could not sail. We beat her on and off the wind quite easily. She was owned, I learned later, by a former Royal Canadian Air Force flyer, an awfully nice fellow. He could be seen around the Club Maritime of Palma in his white turtle-neck sweater with an enormous pair of binoculars hanging from his neck. What he expected to see through these binoculars, heaven only knows, for most of his time was spent on a bar stool, a large glass of gin in hand. True, he would go outside from time to time and lovingly inspect his ship, moored not more than half a cable away, through the wonderful binoculars.

The entrance to the Danforth is easy except the last part where the Club Nautico jetty begins. There, a ship under sail has little space to maneuver, and a slight error in judgment might lead to endless trouble. I have a horror of maneuvering in congested waters, especially when the wind is diverted by tall buildings around the harbor, and one never knows from where the next puff will come. On this occasion, however, all went well, and we dropped the hook at just the right moment, the sails came in, and the secretary of the club, who was just rowing across the harbor in a little dinghy, took our mooring warp while wishing us a most hearty welcome.

It was three-thirty p.m. when we had the vessel secured and everything shipshape on deck. We were then twenty-six days out of Tunis and just halfway to Gibraltar. The distance made good was a little over four hundred miles, but we had sailed in excess of eight hundred fifty. We were greatly behind our planned schedule. Little did we know the delay would save our lives. Three great gales struck the western Mediterranean between December 11 and 22.

Had we not been delayed on the coast of Algeria, and had I been able to keep to my sailing timetable, we would not have survived. The hand of Providence interfered with my plans, and fortunately so, for otherwise I would have sailed my ship and her crew to destruction.

We moored at the principal jetty below the magnificent clubhouse, next to a large motor yacht from England. There was a rush below to change into shore-going outfits, and the small cabin became littered with sea clothing as we pealed off layers of oilskins, sweaters, woolen shirts and sea boot stockings. Mark was first ashore, attired in his best number one jeans, leather jacket, yellow scarf and red and white woolen cap. Bep donned a smart nylon zip coat. I put on my standard shore-going outfit: gray flannels, navy blue blazer and a tie.

We were bursting with enthusiasm, the misery of the North African coastline all but forgotten. Fresh in our minds was the wonderful passage from Collo. Ahead lay the prospect of several days in one of the most beautiful islands of the Mediterranean. This was adventure. This was small boat voyaging at its best. The sun came out. The air was balmy. At that moment there was not one single worry to cloud our horizon. I shut my mind to all problems and, as always, I did not let anything spoil the joy of the first day ashore.

The harbor was crowded with yachts of all sizes and shapes. There was Errol Flynn's *Zaca* from San Francisco, a magnificent black schooner one hundred eighteen feet on deck. She had come to Tunis that summer under charter to some Americans from Maine. There was the large wishbone ketch *Nike Primero,* a beautiful steel vessel eighty feet on deck, all white. She also had been in Tunis. There was *Black Swan*, a forty-foot Newporter hailing from Los Angeles. She was offered for sale following the death of her owner, the actor Tyrone Power, who passed away while filming in Madrid. Later on, her skipper, Capt. Mike Steckler, showed us this splendid ship. She was outfitted with all possible gadgets. There were scores of lesser boats a detailed inspection of which we left for the morrow.

We saw many cargo schooners and other beautiful, well-kept ships, their black or white hulls resembling big yachts. Along one quay we discovered half a dozen old, abandoned small vessels, mostly wartime patrol ships or subchasers that passed into private hands at the end of the war and for many years had indulged in such traffic as cigarettes and other luxury goods which were cheap in Tangier and Gibraltar and worth their weight in gold in Spain and Italy. They were now rotting here, dreaming perhaps of their adventurous careers. Most of them still had their home ports painted on the sterns. Some hailed from England, but the majority came from Gibraltar, which, I was to learn some months later, was still the home port for many such vessels. Smuggling was apparently going as strong as ever, a highly organized and specialized business.

We hung around our ship for ten minutes waiting for someone to come and see our papers, but there was no one in sight. "There is no hurry," said the secretary. "They will be here tomorrow. You just go ahead and make yourself at home." We did just that.

We kicked off with drinks at the clubhouse, beer, Coca-Cola, coffee and all that. How delicious is the first glass of beer ashore – then off to town.

How sweet it is to feel terra firma under one's feet after several days on a little tossing craft. Everything ashore seemed new and attractive to us. We made our way through the winding narrow streets of the old town adjacent to the harbor. It was spotlessly clean, with well-stocked small shops kept by smiling people. The sidewalk cafes were full of people emerging from offices for a cup of something and a chat. There were many tourists, and Spanish and American sailors, for both these navies had bases in Palma. We dashed for newsstands where each of us picked his favorite magazines, then some more refreshments, a good meal and movies.

Walking back on board that night we felt happy and supremely satisfied. More plans were made for the coming days:

a visit to the naval museum, the cathedral, the harbor, the shops for souvenirs. Mark was dreaming of a chessboard and a Spanish wineskin he wanted to use as a water bottle. Bep wanted to send something to his friends. I was after a windproof kerosene lamp.

We stood for some time on the jetty looking at our little ship, which had carried us safely through two major storms. A little deep-sea vessel is a touching sight. I, for one, always feel deep gratitude to my ship for her utter devotion to the task and for her unfailing capabilities.

During the next three days we circulated between the boat, the town and the Hotel Nautico, a pleasant place next to the yacht club. We had arranged to have our baths there for the modest sum of twelve pesetas, equivalent to twenty-five American cents. There was any amount of hot water, so we took our turns soaking luxuriously in the full-length tubs. I had shifted my typewriter, paper, charts and notes to the writing room and spent my mornings writing letters and one or two articles about the voyage. Mark was simply everywhere. He had taken out the rubber dinghy and was rowing all over the club's harbor. On the second day, he made friends with some Spanish boys, and in spite of the language barrier, he managed to get along with them, as only children know how. Bep was stowing and restoring the equipment on board, making excursions to town and outside, and looking over ships, for he was after a bigger yacht for himself. We also arranged for the laundry to be done, water tanks filled, sails dried, fresh provisions brought. This was the usual business, done smoothly and without much trouble. We had a long way ahead. This was, after all, only a short stopover.

I had the great pleasure of talking with Marina on the telephone. She called me one morning, and it was a delight to hear her voice. I was apologetic for the unusually long time we were taking over the voyage. She was, as always, encouraging and hopeful. "I am so proud of you all," she said, and I was grateful for her faith in me. I was resolved not to spare any efforts in bringing the voyage to a successful conclusion. Moreover, I felt I had a duty toward the Tunisian flag we were flying. If we succeeded, *Tethys* would be the first Tunisian ship to cross the Atlantic. There was no room for failure. I was sure of that.

On the third day I began to fret. The novelty of the harbor was wearing off. I was eager to press on. After all, we embarked upon a serious voyage, and while Palma was a most delightful port of call, our purpose was to reach America. I began to make frequent visits to the yacht club where the meteorological bulletins were posted. I talked with old mariners to hear their opinions of what the weather would do. It was a most exceptional year, they agreed. It had rained for forty days, a thing the oldest man could not remember. The winds had been of great violence, and all from the western part.

To digest all this information and collect my thoughts, I took long walks around the yacht harbor. It is the best in western Mediterranean and can take easily one hundred fifty yachts, all moored stern to quay. It is supremely safe and offers all facilities at no charge. The courtesy of the police and customs officials makes it a pleasure to come in. The visitor feels welcome and is treated like an honored guest, not like a nuisance. Mark, when not running somewhere with me, was discussing at length each yacht, her shape, her fittings and rigging. He was fast developing a keen eye for sailing ships and would at once spot the flaws in a design. He knew what made a vessel attractive and what did not. One can learn a lot by such a study of different yachts.

On Sunday we went to the cathedral. The magnificent Gothic structure dates back to the fifteenth century. We sat impressed by the pious atmosphere and the decor. It was a quiet mass, but even so the ceremony was most elaborate. There were five priests and half a dozen attendants in traditional robes. My thoughts wandered to the other great cathedrals of the Mediterranean I had known in my ten years of travel through that inland sea: the twin-dome Benghazi Cathedral in Libya where Mark was christened by the Bishop of Cyrenaica; the little Tripoli Cathedral; the somber, massive building of Genoa; and the cheerful church of Gibraltar, which I was to see again. But my favorite was the Cathedral of the Knights of Malta, St. John's in Valetta. In my six visits to Malta, I never failed to pray in this church so rich in tradition. The nave is surrounded by the chapels of the Catholic kings, and the floor is made of the knights' coats of arms. I liked to walk there meditating about the past and the brave knights, defenders of the faith.

I began to feel the anxiety I always have when the hour of departure draws close. It is a mixture of a desire to be on the way, with a slight fear of the unknown. I felt it more strongly this time, for some strange reason. Looking at Mark so happy, so trusting, I began to have doubts whether I had the right to risk his young life. But then, I reasoned, my boat had proved herself to be supremely seaworthy, and I was more than ever confident of Bep's and my own ability to cope with whatever might happen. Mark was enjoying the experience and was as eager as ever to sail, although he felt happy in this wonderful port of call. I confess I was being a little egotistical, for I wanted so much to have him with us. He was an ideal companion, happy, willing and courageous. Without him much of the pleasure of the voyage would have gone.

The forecast was not particularly good, so I decided to stay one more day to see how the weather would develop. There were no gale warnings for the western Mediterranean, but I thought it a good precaution. On the other hand, I believe I was fully justified in wanting to put to sea. It is foolhardy and unseaman-like to sail in the face of an imminent gale, but in long-distance cruising in small crafts, one cannot afford to be unduly influenced by the possibility of bad weather. The sea is no place for the timid and indecisive.

After a month together, the crew of *Tethys* was a well-trained and harmonious team. Getting under way was performed quietly and without effort. To a casual observer ashore, we must have looked like a yacht going out for an afternoon sail in the bay. But an experienced sailor would at once have recognized *Tethys* for what she was: a deep-sea ship. The baggy wrinkles, the vertical cut mainsail, the cockpit hood and dodgers, the gear neatly stowed on deck and properly lashed, all this signaled that she was engaged upon a deep water voyage.

Mark cast off the stern mooring warps and was the last to jump on board. We had her short on the anchor and set the mainsail. The holding ground was excellent, and we had to join forces to break out the seventeen-pound Danforth. What a marvelous anchor it is. As we began to gather way, I took a last look around the harbor. Mrs. Lighttoller, whom we had met during our stay, was on the foredeck of her motor yacht *Sundowner* waiving good-bye. She knew we were going across the Atlantic and was a little apprehensive that I should take Mark with me on such an adventure. We cheerfully responded to this friendly gesture, waved back, and I turned around, my mind already set on the problems of the passage which lay ahead. And so we put to sea once more bound for Gibraltar. It was December 9, a month and a day out of Tunis.

There was a fresh northerly when we got out of the Palma harbor and set course toward Cape Figueroa, less than ten miles distant. After that, it would be a straight run for Ibiza, the third largest island of the Balearic group.

It is most satisfying to make good progress in the beginning of a passage, and the fast spinning log filled my heart with pleasant anticipation of a quick run to the Cape Palos on the Spanish coast only two hundred miles away, and about halfway to Gibraltar. A fast run – that's what I was hoping for – but fate was to interfere again, and two and half months were to go by before I saw that cape: alone!

Unless the weather is perfect, I never enjoy the first day at sea. Even a few days in port suffice to upset the system, which needs some time to adjust again to constantly rolling and pitching of a small boat. Your thoughts are still full of impressions of the land, and the next port of call is too far off. Appetites are usually poor. As it was midafternoon, we only ate a brief snack in the cockpit after which Mark turned in and Bep kept busy stowing away various odds and ends which were still lying around.

At sea I kept watch with Bep, but the length of the watch varied with conditions. In normal weather, the schedule was four hours on and four off, two-day watches from four to six and six to eight. I also experimented with five- and six-hour tricks at the helm, but we found four hours below enough to get a good rest. In hard going we would change every two hours or even every hour. On especially difficult occasions we both remained on deck, more for moral support to each other than anything else, for *Tethys* was easily handled by one man. Of course, such maneuvers as reefing or taking in sails were much better done by the full crew.

That afternoon I took the first dog-watch and passed the two hours observing the coastline. Beautiful as it is, it looked sad and gray in the December afternoon light. I was trying to decide whether to pass north of Ibiza, or go through the Formentera channel which was a shorter way, but I was not sure of the currents there. Having no engine, I always tried to avoid tight spots. In the Mediterranean one never knows what the weather will do next and I, for one, am unable to predict the conditions an hour in advance.

When I came on deck again for the eight to midnight watch, we were well past the cape. Bep was steering for Ibiza. There were three lights in sight which gave me a good fix. A calm was setting in. There was a swell, and the ship rolled uneasily, slapping her sails. I thoroughly dislike such conditions but could only make the best of the dying breeze. An hour later a complete calm had set in; it did not improve my mood. To be becalmed within sight of land is, to put it mildly, unsettling. You watch the same landmarks hour after hour, and you wonder how long you will be there. It is especially maddening at the beginning or the end of a passage. Once far off at sea, one accepts such conditions with a lighter heart.

All that night we hardly moved, and when daylight broke, a faint breeze began to stir the mirror like surface of the sea. It came from the east, putting Ibiza to windward, but it was better than no wind at all. By midmorning it had strengthened a little and we began the painful business of working to windward. There was a northeasterly current so we hardly made any progress on our long tracks. But there is no other choice in a sailing vessel without power. You have to arm yourself with patience. A small gaff-rigged yacht is hardly the boat to go to windward in a choppy sea, especially if there is any current against you. I kept her well full and by to maintain speed, and we sailed south-southwest, the best course we could lay. Motion is violent when going to windward, and life is far from pleasant. There was little conversation that day, we ate our meals in silence, and the man off watch would promptly turn in to seek some comfort in sleep.

We beat all that day and all night. Towards three a.m. I raised the light of Ibiza. It must have been over fifteen miles distant so I decided to tack and head north-northwest. The wind had freshened. I took a reef without calling Bep on deck. Weather conditions were deteriorating visibly, and I was disgusted. In thirty-six hours we had barely made good thirty miles. Now with the increasing wind there was little hope of doing better. All I could count on was maintaining our position for the time being. A couple of hours later we were rail down, and it was time for the second reef. I kept the two headsails on, for without the jib a cutter like *Tethys* is most ineffective on the wind. The barometer had fallen, and the wind was constantly increasing. The sea, as is usual in the Mediterranean, began to build up fast. The action was short and violent. *Tethys* labored heavily as we tried to push her to windward. The visibility was not too bad, for we could see plainly the northern tip of Ibiza ten miles to windward. It was so near it seemed to us that in spite of everything we could reach it and find some shelter in its lee. The wind kept piping up. By late morning we had the ship under close-reefed mainsail and the storm staysail. We still sailed her to windward, but I was rapidly losing hope of reaching the island.

At midday it was blowing a full gale and we hove her to, for it was no longer possible to force her to windward. She suffered too much. At that point I had a long discussion with Bep as to our tactics. Bep had suggested we run for Palma, but I judged the sea to be too dangerous. I decided to ride it out the best we could. We had unlimited sea room to leeward, so I thought it would be better to try to maintain the position. And, thank heaven, we were out of all shipping lanes!

Soon after, the close-reefed main had to come in and she hove to under the little storm staysail of only fifteen square feet. She lay to like the good little ship she was but began to drift to leeward. It was heartbreaking to watch Ibiza, the only possible shelter, disappearing in the distance. We were in for it, and this time I feared it would be long painful and dangerous. I kept my worries to myself and tried to appear to my crew confident and tough, but I was far from that. The wind had gone to the west-southwest, and it was obvious that it was not just a local disturbance. The whole eastern Atlantic was affected and the western part of the Mediterranean too. It was December 11 when we began our eastward drift, our third major gale since we had left Tunis just over a month ago. The Mediterranean was definitely proving a tough proposition. When setting out on the voyage I envisaged bad weather but never suspected that we would meet such extreme conditions. The elements seemed determined not to let us pass, and a small boat is simply powerless in the face of a sixty-knot storm.

To say that my morale was low is an understatement. I did not even have the feeble comfort of knowing that the gale was driving us on our way. On the contrary, each passing hour was setting us back from whence we came. It was heartbreaking, discouraging, disappointing. But there was nothing to be done. Conditions had to be met and accepted. We had no way out, except to fight for it and hope for the best.

All of the next day, December 12, the wind kept at a steady sixty knots. The sea continued to build. This time there was no heavy rain to check the breaking crests. We were frequently sprayed half way up the mast, but *Tethys* rode remarkably well, and I began to be hopeful. All would be well, providing the wind did not increase. There was no reason for a watch on deck, so we all lived below trying to organize ourselves the best we could. Meals were prepared and eaten fairly regularly, simple meals. Cooking was not an easy task, but the gimbaled primus stove was well able to produce a hot dish even in those difficult conditions. I broke out the best food we had on board, chicken with dumplings, asparagus, many different kinds of canned fruit. We drank hot cocoa. I moved into the forward bunk letting Mark sleep in mine where he could play with the receiver and read more easily, for the gimbaled kerosene lamp was hung close over my bunk. What a delight this lamp was. We kept it going all night, for there is nothing more dismal than a dark cabin on a stormy night. There was constant music pouring out from one of the radios, Bep's portable or the Homer receiver. It was strange to listen to our favorite programs and think of these people ashore safe and comfortable while we were here at sea, three frightened human beings, praying for the storm to abate.

Mark's chessboard, bought in Palma, was a great morale booster. While I preferred to doze or read, Bep and Mark played one game after another. Seeing their concentration one could hardly believe a full storm raged around us. Another favorite game was Naval Battle in which Mark became quite an expert.

Tethys was lying nearly broadside on the little storm staysail set to keep her steady. The sea was high, short and breaking, but our drift to leeward was still producing a smooth spot, which flattened the crests before they could reach us. Only spray was coming on board. *Tethys* was behaving well. I had no qualms providing the wind did not increase. We even began to joke about the weather. Mark pretended to be a lift operator calling out as we rose on a sea, "Going up; third floor, fourth, fifth, sixth, up, up, up top floor, ladies and gentlemen, going down," and we would rush down on the other side of the steep watery mountain.

There was not much change in the weather all that day and the following night. The sea was building up, but it also began to lengthen. Sailing our small craft became somewhat easier. However, this improvement was deceiving and temporary. I knew we'd be entering the gale's third stage when the long seas gained in height. Then they would break dangerously, and the broadside position would not be safe any longer.

47

I kept a careful record of our drift, which I estimated at thirty miles a day to the northeast. Entries in the log were made every hour except at night when I recorded the weather conditions every four hours. Otherwise, there was little we could do but try to keep our morale up and wait.

December 13. The beginning of the third day of the storm was sunny and cold. The glass was very low, the wind over seventy-nine knots. The sea viewed from the low deck of *Tethys* presented a magnificent but terrifying spectacle. It was dark blue in the morning light, long white crests stood out sharply against the sky rolling with great speed, their tops carried by vicious blasts in long streams of foam and spray. Solid water was coming on deck. *Tethys* lay flat on her side at times, but her ton of ballast gave her good stability, and she came up easily shaking off water from her decks. Considering the state of the sea, her motion was kind and easy on the crew because her ballast was partly inside and well cemented to the bilges. I was full of admiration for my little ship. Never before have I seen a boat so steady and sea-kindly and gentle in her movements.

After half an hour on deck I had no doubt that we were reaching the climax of the gale. I was in doubt as to what to do next, so I decided to wait and see and keep the little storm staysail on. The helm was lashed well down and she rode about seven points off the wind, which was just a little better than being completely broadside on. She would pay off before the more vicious gusts but then would come back to her position.

The ship's company was not talkative that morning. We breakfasted in silence on hot tea and bread with jam. Then we all turned in to our bunks to while away the morning. I picked up a paperback novel I was reading since our shakedown cruise to Malta and tried to concentrate on it, but my mind was too uneasy. I found it impossible to relax. The hours dragged on, the wind increasing. The breaking sea made an unpleasant noise. *Tethys* was no longer riding easily.

Came midday and I asked Bep and Mark whether they wanted to eat. There was not much enthusiasm for food. We were too tense to think of eating. Now and again one of us would crack a joke to relieve the tension. I could not help admiring my crew for their self-control and calm.

Soon after noon several big seas came on board in quick succession, and the brave little *Tethys* struggled a long time to recover. At one p.m. we were hit by an exceptionally violent sea which broke right across the foredeck sending cataracts of water through the supposedly watertight fore hatch right above the lee bunk where I lay. "That was a big one," Mark said and went on reading. It was a fair warning of what was to follow. Ten minutes later, we heard a big sea approaching. A breaking sea makes a lot of noise, a hissing sound for which I don't care much. I cannot help listening and wondering whether it will break to windward or strike the ship. This one was not hissing. It was roaring like a waterfall combined with thunder.

"There it comes," shouted Mark.

"Hold on, boys," shouted Bep.

And then it came! I felt the ship go up and up and up, heeling over all the time on the steep wall of the sea. There was a deafening blow as the comber struck us and rolled us on the beam. We went crushing down, carried by the angry crest, hitting the sea to leeward with our port side heeled over ninety degrees. The ship shook. I was violently thrown against the shelf above my bunk. Rope and other equipment securely wedged on the other side shot across in a heap on top of me as I made an effort to struggle over the canvas lee guard. In the main cabin, I saw Bep already out of his bunk. Mark was covered with books and other odds and ends which came flying across from Bep's bunk. *Tethys* was still on her side. "On deck," I cried, not quite knowing what I should do there! "Come up, for heaven's sake, come up," I prayed, making my way to the main hatch. Bep was by then halfway through. I followed on his heels, and we shot up on deck. The monstrous sea was well to leeward. A smooth wave followed, as always, after a big one, but another steep sea was building up not far to windward. It was on us by the time we reached the mast. Bep crouched down by the windward rigging.

I jumped up on the boom and wound my arms and legs around the mast. It was a big one all right, but it broke to windward, and although we got tons of solid water on deck, much of its momentum was spent before it had reached us.

The broadside position was now dangerous. Something had to be done to keep her head to wind. Otherwise, one more sea like that could roll us right over and send us to the bottom. I shivered at the thought of it.

We still carried the storm staysail, which was taken off at once. We brought out two sixty-fathom warps and streamed them from the starboard bow with two old jibs at the end to act as anchor.

The jib and staysail were unbent and stowed below. Halyards were secured near the mast. We also took out the compass and stowed it safely in Mark's bunk. The staysail boom, although securely lashed on deck, was snapped like a "rotten carrot," as Mark said later. A loose coil of rope stowed between the mast and the cabin was hanging half way up the ratlines. The lee lifeline stanchions, which carried the canvas dodger, were bent six inches inboard when the ship fell on her side.

We stayed on deck for a while to see how she would ride now. I wanted to stream the warps by the stern, but Bep was of the opinion that it was safer to ride by the bow. She now lay six points off the wind which was not too bad. We retired below to put some order and rest. Under such conditions, half an hour's work can be quite exhausting.

Some sugar was passed around as we lay below in silence listening to the moaning wind and the hissing sea. I knew we had reached knock-down conditions, and from now on there was real danger to the ship. The unlimited sea room was of some comfort, but I did not know how long these conditions would last. The glass was terribly low. There was no sign of any improvement. We did what we could for the ship. From there on everything was in the hands of God. I lay in the fore bunk all afternoon, calculating whether to risk running with warps astern if the conditions deteriorated further. *Tethys* with her strong construction could take a lot of beating, but her low freeboard and consequently little reserve buoyancy were not a guarantee that a freak wave would not run her right under. I finally decided against this extreme measure. We were better lying six points off the wind, the warps and the improvised sea anchor giving enough hold and at the same time allowing her to drift at a comfortable rate. Moreover, the chances were that we would not encounter a second time the precise conditions when the roll of the ship coincides with a heavy breaking sea.

Nothing happened until eight p.m. when two enormous waves knocked us down on our ear, but they were not as dangerous as the noon ones. Providing the cabin held, *Tethys* would float through it all. I was confident, for she was built around four stout posts reaching right down to the frames.

During the night the sea built up to a great height, but it also began to lengthen. I estimated that the Mediterranean had reached its grandest mood, and I was impressed. The seas were about twenty-four feet high. I didn't suppose the Mediterranean could produce more than that. To be sure it was quite enough. I really didn't care for more!

Going on deck at midnight, I saw two small steamers dodging slowly into the gale. I am always surprised to meet other ships in the emptiness of the sea. They were more than a mile off so we showed no lights.

Bep lay in his bunk with the portable radio on his chest, trying to drown the noise of the sea in the lively music coming over the airwaves from an all-night station in Paris. Mark slept peacefully wedged with cushions and blankets against the motion. I crawled back to the fore bunk, my body aching, my morale sagging.

December 14 saw no improvement in the weather. By a strange coincidence, we were again knocked down between noon and one p.m. and eight and nine in the evening. It was the last big sea of the storm, but it hit us with tremendous violence across the starboard quarter, and we flew from one tack to the other, the bow held by the streamed warps. The dodger took most of the blow. Two stanchions were bashed more than a foot inboard nearly to the cabin side. I thanked God none of us were on deck, for it would have meant death or grave injury to be caught by such a blow.

Tethys refused to go back to the starboard tack, and the warps were now cutting under the bobstay which, although it was of chain, would have cut across the two warps in less than an hour. Bep performed a superhuman effort in heaving in the whole works and streaming it on the port bow. We hastily rigged the canvas dodger which was torn off on that side. It is strange how very exposed and defenseless we felt without that strip of canvas.

December 15 and 16 went by. The gale was raging, but there were lulls and the sea lost some of its power. We had by then drifted some one hundred eighty miles to the east-northeast. In better moments we would crawl on deck to seek some warmth in the pale winter sun. We were depressed, and even Mark did not joke as usual. Bep's unshaven face was drawn and gray. Mark looked much thinner. I wear a full beard at all times which, I like to imagine, gives me a wolfish appearance, but my crew firmly declared I looked far from the tough mariner I was supposed to be!

December 17 and our seventh day of gale, dawned gray and uninviting but the sea was considerably calmer and the barometer was rising. By late morning the sea was only moderate but still too much to think of beating towards Minorca, now the nearest shelter eighty miles to the northeast. I did not know our exact position, and all that day there was no sun to take a position from. I estimated that we had drifted two hundred miles since December 11, but it was only a guess.

That afternoon we had a pleasant surprise. Bep and Mark were playing the Naval Battle game, and I was hopefully cleaning the sextant when we all lifted our heads to an unfamiliar sound. "Thunder," I said bending over my precious instrument, "but it does sound a bit odd." Bep listened attentively for a moment then declared firmly, "I am positive it's gunfire."

Mark's interest was immediately aroused by such possibility and he was first to jump for the companion. I was close behind him. The first thing we saw was a target towing aircraft.

"Well," I said, "there must be a carrier somewhere," and sure enough there was one not two miles away to the northeast. Fighters were taking off, and three escorting destroyers were blazing away at the target. Quite a little action. Mark was in raptures at such unexpected and wonderful entertainment.

"I have never seen an aircraft carrier before," he kept repeating in fascination. He could hardly take his eyes off the big ship, which seemed not to be affected at all by the sea. She steamed into the wind sending her fighters into the air. We dressed in oilskins and took our cameras out to try to put the scene on film.

A helicopter flew low over us, and I was tempted to ask for some rope, but I was afraid my signals might be taken for a request for assistance. We waved greetings instead. We stayed on deck for a good hour when at last the squadron faded in the early December dusk. It was strange to think that the men on board would enjoy movies and hot showers that evening, while we were faced with another stormy night at sea and a long beat to Minorca.

The meeting provided subject for conversation for the rest of the evening, and as the weather was definitely improving, we were in rather good mood. There was a fair prospect of a better day on the morrow. We lay in our bunks that night listening to music, resting and hoping. It was our seventh day hove to, and I thought we deserved a break. I knew it would not be easy to beat back the eight miles to Minorca. Really we should have started sailing that night, but we were exhausted. I wanted a full night's sleep for all of us. Bep mumbled something about setting sail, but I pretended not to hear and drifted off into a restful strength-giving sleep.

On the afternoon of December 18, there was a fresh southwesterly, and *Tethys* full under a reefed main and two headsails was making good time towards the Spanish island of

Minorca. What a wonderful sensation to be sailing again after seven days of drifting and tossing out of control. We had spent the morning clearing up the mess on deck, bedding sails. The two warps were hauled in, and in what state they were! The old jibs were chafed and torn. The warps were unlaid and twisted in knots on nearly half their length. Both were brand new, a two-inch manila and a two-and-a-half-inch sisal!

I was able to fix our position by sun and moon observations, and it coincided remarkably with my dead reckoned estimate. We were just over eighty miles from Minorca and well over two hundred miles from our position of December 11. We stood watch that day and the following night, pressing as much as we could. It was rough going and tiring for the crew, but all we were thinking of was shelter. The safety of a port was what we dreamed of during that beat to the same islands we had left ten days ago, so hopefully, for Gibraltar.

The wind kindly backed towards the southern sector, and we were able to make a course a little north of west towards the northeasterly tip of Minorca. When daylight came on the second day of our beat, Bep was on deck, binoculars in hand, checking on my navigation. I had no great qualms about the result of my calculations, but he seemed to doubt that we would ever see dry land again. It was his trick at the helm. I could see him from below standing on the cockpit seat steering with his feet binoculars glued to his face. I knew we were within ten miles of land and that it should come in sight at any moment, for visibility was good.

I was deep in the study of the "Sailing Directions" when Bep called us on deck and announced with pride, as if he just made a great discovery, "There she is." Indeed there she was, the rocky island of Minorca, six miles to the southwest. I at once called a conference to decide on our tactics. There were but two possibilities: Port Mahon on the eastern side or Port Fornells on the northern. We were northeast of the island, the wind was from the southwest, and both these ports were twelve miles to windward. We decided to head half-way between the two places, so that we could reach one of them easily if the wind changed. If it did not, we would have the same distance to sail in any case. "Well, boys, there will be beer and Coca-Cola tonight!" I exclaimed with a feeling of satisfaction. I could see us sitting down to a good dinner ashore. After all we had but a few miles to go. But there was no beer that night or the next.

The day was spent beating towards land, the choppy sea made progress slow and extremely painful. To make good three miles we had to sail fifteen! We tacked patiently all day and part of the night. Bep and I stayed on deck, for our nerves were too strained to relax. A gale warning came over Radio Monte Carlo. My spirits sank. "Heavens, not another storm," I thought with dismay. "Haven't we had our share already?"

Fourteen days of storms in a month and half were more than I had bargained for. At eleven that night we were closing in on land north of Port Fornells. The island afforded some shelter, but now we had the disadvantage of darkness. The entrance to the bay of Fornells is easy when you know it. In total darkness it looks forbidding and dangerous. We raced against the setting moon to have the benefit of her guiding light. We had entered strange ports at night many times before, but this was a bay with unknown currents and perhaps rocks. We beat towards the light to the west of the bay's entrance. Cutting across the entrance to the bay, we could clearly see the two leading lights flashing rapidly. I really had no heart to risk coming in. Bep sensed my feeling, and I was grateful when touching my shoulder with an assuring gesture, he said, "Look here, why don't we heave to till daylight?"

"Bep, you took it out of my mouth," I said with relief. "Let's reef her right down and sail on and off the coast as close as we can. We're under the lee of land, and it shouldn't be too uncomfortable."

Bep has a powerful constitution. His resistance to discomfort and fatigue is superior to mine. He offered to stand the first watch. I threw myself gratefully onto his bunk. It was bitterly cold. I was shivering and exhausted. The fatigue began to tell on me. I was thankful to see Mark dry and warm and fast asleep in his bunk.

I took over at three a.m. We had drifted two miles from the coast. I should have made an effort to sail her back, but I couldn't face three hours at the helm. I spent my watch warming my backside over the primus stove sipping tea. I had lost a great amount of calories, and it was important to recuperate. We were not yet in port, and there were signs in the sky that another blow was coming.

We went on deck at seven. It was already blowing hard. We had drifted four miles from land. Now with the close-reefed main and the staysail, we started to beat our way back hoping to get close to the entrance of the bay before the full force of the gale struck. The sky to windward was black and evil looking. The spectacle was frightening. Our weakened condition and low morale did not help with facing the coming danger. There was no question of trying to enter the bay. All we could do was to come as close to the island as possible to seek some shelter from the sea, which even at such close distance from land was full of fury and power.

The first squall hit us just before eight. It was wicked beyond imagination. It became dark. The clouds seemed to touch wave tops, which were now completely white and hitting with such power and violence that I thought we would break into bits and pieces at any moment. We kept the close-reefed main and the staysail on. Both were of twelve-ounce Egyptian cotton and brand new. But the force of the wind was such that I thought it impossible they would resist. I was especially worried about the staysail. It was under terrific pressure and would blow to ribbons with any sudden shift of wind. We were nearly flat on our lee side, the coast now obliterated by the rain, spray and clouds. The scene was of such desolation that I could stand it no longer. It was December 11 repeated all over. We were being driven from land once more by a raging storm even more violent than the one which drove us from Ibiza. I feared for the safety of the sails and the mast. We could not beat any longer. The staysail had to be taken in. Even Bep, who was the very devil when it came to driving to windward, agreed that it was time to heave to under the shortest canvas we could muster.

With the small storm staysail set, *Tethys* became immediately easier in her movements. She kept nicely her station, shipping only occasional water across her weather bow. I ordered us all below to rest. The squalls kept marching one after another all that dismal day. We three were rapidly approaching the limit of our moral endurance. I felt a great physical weariness coming over me. My mental powers could no longer provide the driving force to combat fatigue, pessimism and disgust with the weather, the ship and my surroundings. I kept my face straight, to be sure. I did not let Bep and Mark see how very low I felt. It was bitter to think that I dragged Mark into it all – that we were again being driven away from land and that we should perhaps have to spend Christmas at sea.

The night that followed was the worst of the whole trip. Although the gale was easing off, there was yet no question of sailing her. We had drifted twenty miles to the north of Port Fornells. I lay between the bunks on the cabin sole exhausted and wet with my feet under the companion steps in the cold bilge water. I was half-asleep, shivering all over. I heard Bep get up in the middle of the night. It must have been two a.m. He let me lie there, and I was grateful, for I don't think I would have had enough stamina to go on deck and set sail. That night I was as close to acknowledging defeat of my undertaking as I will ever want to be. How could we possibly succeed in getting to Gibraltar against such odds? I no longer had the will to press on. I was no longer thinking of my sailing schedule. All I wanted was to get to some harbor and rest and sleep. It was a bitter night. I was near losing faith in my ability to sail a small ship across the sea. Was I to be beaten? Was I to surrender?

Bep was on deck setting sails. I knew he could handle *Tethys* himself, and I let him do it. I could tell by the motion of the boat when he set the staysail and then the jib, for poor *Tethys* staggered like a drunken man under the pressure of canvas. She kept her lee deck constantly under, shuddering, shaking and suffering. I did not care any longer. Surely Bep will sail the stick right out of her poor tortured body, I thought, but I did not care.

He let me stay below. I did not move until daylight. I dragged my aching body to the cockpit and looked in silence at Bep. His deeply lined face was greenish blue with exhaustion and cold. A ten-day-old beard gave him a wild appearance. But he stuck grimly to the helm determined to get her to port. I sat for a long while collecting my wits.

"Go and lie down, Bep," I said. "I will take her now. Thank you for letting me sleep." He stood up without a word and slowly slid down the companion.

With my hand on the tiller, I felt *Tethys* respond to the pressure of her rudder. I felt great tenderness in my heart for this brave little ship, so faithful. I bent over to read the compass course and settled down to beat across the island once more.

CHAPTER FIVE

Senor Caules greeted me with a cheerful "buenos dias" as I descended the stairs of the little hotel. I stopped to exchange a few words with this kind old man, who since our invasion of his place that Sunday afternoon of December 21, took such good care of us. The big square dining room was empty. It was winter and we were the only guests. The dozen or so tables were covered with equipment we had taken out of *Tethys*. Half a dozen sails were piled up in a corner, along with blankets, clothing, sea bags, charts, books, notes and typewriter. We kept one table free for meals and playing chess.

As I sat down to await breakfast, my eyes traveled across the small harbor where *Tethys* lay securely moored by her bow to the stone jetty with two anchors at the stern. For the hundredth time since coming in to this wonderful bay of Fornells, my mind went back to events of the last few days.

After successfully weathering the severe storm of December 11 to 17 and again on the 20th, we came near disaster in the very harbor of Fornells. It was late afternoon when we sailed into the peaceful haven of this little fishing port, feasting our eyes on the white houses and green slopes of surrounding hills. Boys and girls ran along the shore excited by the unexpected arrival of our boat. Fishermen in their Sunday best, stood in groups looking with curiosity at the little ship which chose to travel in the seas in such an unlikely season. They were men experienced in the ways of small boats and were well aware of the dangers of the winter gales.

It was a great moment of relief when our Danforth anchor rattled out touching the sandy bottom after twelve days and five hundred miles of stormy seas. I was so eager to tie her up, that, unwisely, I chose the leeward berth in the small enclosed harbor which was itself landlocked inside the bay. The entrance was less than a cable wide and opened to the north. As we dropped the hook to windward, it was much easier to fall back with the wind letting out the cable. The depth was two fathoms with good holding ground, and with sixty fathoms out, we rode to a thirty to one scope. We had her moored in less than ten minutes and were ready when the authorities arrived to board the vessel. The formalities were more of a welcome than control. After wishing us a happy Christmas and a pleasant stay, the policeman and the harbor master took themselves off discretely.

That night we established our headquarters in Senor Caules' little hotel, a pleasant two-story building at the head of the harbor, screened by a row of short, well-developed palms. We took a double room. It was agreed that Bep and I would sleep in turn on board. Mark was granted the privilege of staying ashore all the time. We drew lots for the first night, and it fell to me to remain on board.

With another gale warning that night from the southwest, I was grateful for the calm day we had been granted which allowed us to reach the safety of this harbor. Providence or a lucky star, call it what you wish, was with us all the time on this voyage. Had we not been delayed by two gales off the coast of Algeria, the great blow we had just gone through would have caught us somewhere near Spain, or perhaps already in the Atlantic, and I doubt whether we would have survived without sea room. Now another storm was brewing. It was to be the severest of all.

Many lives were lost in the two days that followed. A Spanish trawler foundered with all hands, and an English yacht was bashed to pieces near Algeria on the southern coast of Spain taking the life of Dr. Nielsen of the famous Norwegian yacht

Stavanger, then lying at Gibraltar. In Oran, winds exceeded ninety knots. The Straits of Gibraltar recorded gusts of one hundred twelve knots. Big ships were breaking mooring lines in ports. Torrential rains flooded Western Europe and North Africa. The hand of Providence had guided our little ship and her crew through all these perils. I am inclined to believe that our seamanship played only a minor role in keeping us alive.

That night, from force of habit, I kept the cabin light on. For a long while I lay in my bunk listening to the peaceful ticking of the clock, my eyes wandering along the familiar objects of this little cabin which was to be my home for eight months.

The unfamiliar movement of the boat dancing to the short harbor chop shook me out of my deep sleep. It was broad daylight. The noise of the waves slapping against the topside alerted my mind to the fact that I was lying onto a leeward quay and that likely my presence was required on deck. An unpleasant thought when the bunk is nice and warm and it is blowing outside!

Under the pressure of wind, which was now at least force seven, *Tethys* had drifted on the quay which was now no more than a couple of feet off the stern. I heaved on the anchor cable and busied myself setting bowlines to ease the strain. After that she held her head firmly into the wind, and I had no qualms about leaving her alone. The anchor cable was a stout manila I had brought from Malta. The anchor was our trusty Danforth.

Bep and Mark were still lazing in bed, the chessboard in between their beds when I came in. Mark had developed an uncanny passion for that game and found a willing partner in Bep, but the prospect of a long walk into the surrounding hills and exploration of an ancient Roman watchtower aroused both of them. We set out after an early lunch provided by the kind Senor Caules who never tired of watching with deep amazement the speed with which his dishes disappeared into our stomachs. I think he was pleased as well as a little worried at the amount of food we three were able to stow away.

We set out then for a couple of hours to stretch our legs, as it were, and breathe a little of the mountain air we needed after twelve days of sea spray and confinement in the restricted space of *Tethys'* quarters. It was blowing fairly hard, and there definitely was danger of a sudden increase of the strength of wind, but I went on with my habitual trust that nothing bad would happen to us. Well, nothing did, but it was a close shave.

It was just getting on to four in the afternoon when we came back well satisfied with our walk. I settled down in the dining room to write when I saw Bep running towards the hotel from the direction of the ship. I rushed out. Bep was short of breath.

"We'd better set out the other anchor at once. It's blowing hard. She's putting a lot strain on the Danforth. There is not much time."

I did not lose time in useless questions. The wind had indeed strengthened to a full gale during our absence. I could see from where we stood that the anchor cable was taut as an iron bar, and *Tethys* was jerking on it with the full load of her four tons. "Come on," I said curtly.

We ran back to the ship. The wind was now coming in strong gusts, and there was great activity in the harbor. All the fishing population was busy tending their mooring cables, setting out anchors or dragging the boats clear out of the water.

Tethys' stern was less than a foot from the stone jetty. She was tugging viciously at her anchor cable, which was taut as a bar of iron. The bow cables no longer afforded her relief. While I was casting off the bow cables, Bep jumped on board and somehow managed to heave in a fathom or so of the anchor cable, and the distance between the ship and jetty widened. I was preparing to go on board, so I pulled hard on the mooring line. There was a terrible gust of wind. *Tethys* took a violent plunge burying her bowsprit. I felt the warp go slack in my hand, and the ship charged onto the quay. My faith in the Danforth was such that I yelled to Bep, "Cable is gone." I braced myself against the stern pushing it sideways. It was already pounding on the stony quay, and the only salvation was to let her come alongside. "Sails, Bep, sails," I gasped, sick with effort. He understood and threw a bundle of sails which were in the cockpit between the ship and the jetty.

Mark appeared from somewhere and was on board in one jump, pulling cushions from below to act as fenders. Our joint efforts would not have saved the ship from serious damage had not a score of fishermen jumped to our rescue.

By combined efforts, we succeeded in holding her off while a motorboat was being brought to carry a hawser across to the windward side of the harbor. There were half a dozen men now on board *Tethys* getting the ropes in. Finally I understood what had happened to the anchor. The cable had not parted, nor did the Danforth drag. It was simply torn out together with an enormous chunk of bottom clinging to it. Had the anchor cable been all chain, it would not have happened. Only ten fathoms out of six were chain, and the line could not absorb the violent shocks transmitted to the anchor. Moreover, our Danforth was only a seventeen-pounder, whereas the makers recommend a thirty-pound hook for our size boat in stormy conditions. I press this point, for I want to make it quite clear that it was not the anchor that failed. Now, after an eight-month voyage, I do not hesitate to advise Danforth as the best all-around anchor for yachtsmen, especially deep water voyagers to whom space and weight are of paramount importance.

There were drinks for all hands that night at Senor Caules' bar. The folk of Fornells would not think of accepting any payment for their help. It was given with generosity and disregard for any gains as only men of the sea know how to give. I felt very close to these men who stood shyly in a circle, shuffling their feet, embarrassed, holding awkwardly the little glasses in their huge strong hands. I could not help drawing a comparison between these people who made their living out of the sea and the Bedouins, dwellers of the desert. Both were close to nature, generous, hospitable and honest. We shook hands. The gathering broke. I stood there for a long while with a wonderful feeling of confidence in the basic goodness of human nature.

*****

Time went by quickly, and I could not reach any decision as to our future plans. We were so sea weary that the mere idea of having to put to sea again made me shudder. I thought it better to simply wait and see. There was no longer any question of keeping to my original sailing schedule.

Then came Christmas. We had asked Senor Caules for a special dinner. On Christmas morning, Bep and Mark made a shopping expedition to Port Mahon. It was only a twenty-mile drive, but the road was a country lane and the bus a 1932 model, so it took an hour and half with all the stops. In the afternoon, we went to the woods with the ship's axe to cut a suitable tree – there could be no Christmas without one. Some candles were on board, and the cotton wool out of our medical box imitated snow. A few ornaments made of colored paper completed the decorations. It was a poor tree, but it was our tree, and we were proud of it. With the candles lit, we sat around admiring our handicraft, happy to be alive. We exchanged gifts. Bep gave Mark candy and me a smart tie. I had a small bottle of lavender for Bep and more candy for Mark. Mark very thoughtfully bought cigarettes for Bep and pipe tobacco for me. They were poor gifts but all there was to be had in the village of Fornells. Our joy would not have been greater had we been able to offer each other the most expensive presents in the world.

The midnight mass in the whitewashed village church was impressive in its simplicity. The entire population of five hundred was there except for the infants, men on the left, women on the right, all dressed in their very best. I felt much a part of this community. I had a sense of belonging to these people. I was no stranger. These were friends. Yet soon it would be time to go and move west across the vast sea, for our destiny lay on the other side of the ocean. This was but a port of call on a long journey.

We walked back silently, spellbound by the serenity of this Christmas Eve, bound by friendship born in the face of common danger and sealed by the romance of adventure at sea.

CHAPTER SIX

After the great storm of December 22 and 23, the weather finally settled down to a normal Mediterranean winter. Unhappily, the winds kept in the western sector, and I had no heart to set a date for sailing. I announced vaguely to my crew that I intended to stay fifteen days or so, but there was no assurance whatsoever that the stormy period was over. The weather was settled as much as it could ever be in an unpredictable sea like the Mediterranean. We three needed rest and regular food and plenty of sleep. It was not, however, our physical condition that worried me. We were healthy and strong and by now quite used to the hardships of life in a small boat. It was my own despondent state of mind which loomed large as a potential danger to the success of the voyage.

I was cautious not to show my anxiety to Bep and Mark. Bep, to be sure, being an experienced sailor understood well the difficulties we were facing. Mark was enjoying the adventure, but I could sense he was tired of the slow progress we were making. He never, by word or behavior, showed fear or impatience. He was willing to put to sea at any time and stay there for an indefinite period. In port he was especially happy. Everything was new to him. He was busy exploring, rowing in the rubber dinghy, fishing, helping on board. He had discovered in Fornells a new and exciting interest. He was just over twelve. At his age it was especially important that he should get the proper idea what deep water voyaging under sail was. Under the circumstances he might have developed a conviction that it was all rough seas, rain, wind and discomfort. As much as I could, I tried to make fun of our many difficulties and slow progress. We spent one entire evening planning New Year's dinner menu, which, after a long discussion by all hands, was agreed as follows:

Stormy Sea Consommé
Steaks a la Headwind
Tossed Salad (Very much so!)
Souffle Westerly Gale
Windward Passage Cake

After a few days we had seen everything there was to be seen at Fornells and its surroundings. It was a charming place, and we were glad to have come here instead of Port Mahon, which although larger did not have the atmosphere of this fishing village. The population lived off fishing. The three-dozen small craft in the harbor ranged from about twelve feet to thirty. The houses were poor but spotlessly clean. There was no extreme poverty, and it seemed to me that all were more or less on the same economic level. There were few attractions and nothing to excite desire of possessions. There was no race to keep up with the Joneses. The half a dozen ancient motorcars were mainly used as transport for hire for summer visitors. There was but one telephone.

Along the road leading out of the village were several summer houses belonging to wealthier people from the mainland, but at this time of the year they stood empty and quiet. One only, more modest than the others, had an occupant, a foreigner, I was told. I saw him once, the day we were in trouble during the storm when he had come to the harbor to give a hand. A bearded man of pleasing appearance, he disappeared quietly after we were securely moored. I saw him again one evening with his wife and a small boy in the village square. I was most eager to approach this mysterious man but did not dare to intrude on the privacy of those who came maybe to seek peace and quiet in this unspoiled haven of the Mediterranean. Never shall I learn their origin or their names.

The road along the bay and the hills beyond the village became my favorites for late afternoon walks. I felt the need for solitude in which I could seek comfort and strength to carry on. These were my moments of weakness I was determined to conceal from Mark and Bep. I had reached a point where I had to convince myself that I would not fail in getting my ship across the ocean to America. This force I had to acquire within myself. No one could give it to me. The responsibility was mine alone. I had to have moral strength and indestructible belief that I would succeed.

We had now been nearly two months out of Tunis. The miserable four hundred miles we had made good were hardly encouraging. We had actually sailed over one thousand two hundred. There were another five thousand miles to go. I hardly dared think of such a mighty distance. The Spanish coast, only two hundred miles away, appeared almost beyond my range, beyond my strength, out of my reach forever. The six hundred miles to Gibraltar loomed ahead as a fantastic distance which would take months to negotiate.

I walked for hours trying to build up confidence and courage within myself. It was not so much the fear of the sea itself but the realization that I was facing the possibility of defeat which troubled my ego. I saw clearly how easily the sea could beat a man. But then, I reasoned, we had not done so badly after all. We had successfully weathered three major storms. We were healthy. The ship was good. Time was our real loss, and our plans would have to be adjusted to fit the new conditions. As Bep said, it was important to get there, and time should only be a secondary consideration.

As the weather continued calm, we began to think timidly of putting to sea once more. The sailing date, which was set for January 15, was advanced to the 20th. And then one day, we all agreed that the very next fair wind would see us off.

By January 8 we were ready to sail. *Tethys* was loaded with all her equipment and sails. The forestaysail boom had been nicely repaired by a local carpenter for the equivalent sum of

Benghazi, Libya circa 1947

England circa 1944

Tethys in port

Tethys rolling along in the sparkling trades under headsail only in wind force 6

Tethys sailing herself which she did for long periods of time

A breaking sea signals the start of a gale

The Shell Tanker Arca speaking to the Tethys fifty-two days out of Tangier

The cockpit about which the author said; "I lived here"...

The log fouled by Sargasso weed

photos were taken by Christopher and are reproduced here along with the captions from the feature article in "The Rudder" Magazine - Vol. 75 - No.11 Nov. 1959

Balearic Islands 1957

Tethys at anchor

Chris arriving in New York after solo crossing of the Atlantic.

Chris' son Marc

Chris' son Marc

All above photos were taken by Christopher, except the one of himself.

twenty-three cents, and that included four large brass screws which must have cost at least half of that. We singled out our moorings to two ropes and the Danforth anchor. Water tanks were topped up, fresh provisions taken, and we were ready to go.

This time, however, I would not press. We would go as far as possible and make short hops if necessary. I wanted to avoid at all costs being driven back. New tactics had to be used to fight the stubborn Mediterranean. We too could be stubborn and persistent.

There was a faint northeasterly breeze on the morning of January 5 as we moved slowly toward the narrow entrance of the bay. Mark was up in the rigging waving good-bye to his friends. Senor Caules was out in his boat beyond the end of the inner breakwater, seeing us off. We promised ourselves we'd come back one day to this charming spot for a lengthy visit.

We were not a mile out when the wind died, but after ten minutes of complete calm, a breeze sprung up from the west. There were twelve miles to go to the cape along the northern coast of Minorca, and it was now a dead beat. My heart sank. For a moment I hesitated and considered whether to continue or put back. Bep solved the problem, offering to take the first watch. He was full of energy and steered for many hours through that cold January day along the rocky, inhospitable coast of Minorca, refusing to be relieved. I was glad to stay below in the bunk dozing away, feeling lousy in the short violent pitching. We made no lunch but ate some cheese and bread, washing it down with powerful swigs of Scotch. Mark kept invisible all day sleeping soundly, refusing all food. He asked for a glass of lemonade at midday and promptly turned his back again to the whole world.

That day will be remembered as the least pleasant of our Mediterranean voyage. I was thoroughly disgusted by the time I took the helm late in the afternoon. We had logged twenty-five miles to make good ten, and it was now up to me to beat around the cape. The wind had gone to the southwest, presenting us with another beat toward the mountainous island of Majorca, which stood out clearly against the evening sky.

My mind went back to the pleasant shakedown cruise we had made with Mark only three months before. The warm nights under the brilliant Mediterranean moon were still fresh in my memory but now very distant. Where were the sunny delightful days at Malta which Mark liked so much? What a pleasure it was to see his enthusiasm for this strange island he had first seen as a four-month-old baby en route to Libya. A stiffening southwesterly brought me back to reality, and I pondered the advisability of continuing on to Majorca. At eight-thirty I called Bep on deck to take a reef. Wind was fresh, and once around Cape Minorca, we drove into a westerly swell, which did not help our mood. The prospect of an all-night beat towards Minorca had no appeal to our tired bodies. We agreed without much arguing to call at Ciutadella on the island of Minorca eight miles south of the cape. I kept the boat well clear off the coast steering south until ten p.m. when Ciudadela's light came abeam. We then had a downwind run for the entrance. There was no large-scale chart of the harbor on board, and I was a little uneasy. From the "Sailing Directions," I knew that the entrance was about one quarter of a cable wide and that the harbor itself was really a creek a mile long and very narrow.

As we approached, Bep took the helm. I went forward to pilot him in. I have a better than average night vision. We could hear the surf breaking even before seeing the lights, but we were committed to sail in, so I urged Bep to keep a straight course and drive on at very nearly our maximum speed. We had a short argument whether to take off the main and run under headsails to reduce speed, but I was firm in my decision to keep the mainsail on, for if anything went wrong at the last minute we could still beat our way out, perhaps!

There was an anxious moment when only the green light marking the harbor entrance came in view and the noise of breakers became alarmingly near. The next moment, however, the red light also appeared clearly, and we shot into the entrance. We drove on through the winding creek, rocks on both sides.

Buildings towered ahead, and a bridge seemed to end the channel. The whole thing did not look at all like a harbor, and I thought it safer to stop right there, so we let go the anchor, rounded up into the wind, swung toward the stone quay and tied up before one could say knife.

In another moment we had the sails neatly folded, halyards coiled, and I was able to throw myself on my bunk without even bothering to take off the three sweaters and two pairs of pants I wore. My last reaction of the day was a log entry: "11 p.m. tied up at Ciutadella, 14 hours from Fornells, distance sailed: 38 miles, distance made good: 23 miles – I feel positively rotten."

*****

The six days we spent at Ciutadella were pleasant and restful. Formalities like in other Balearic ports were of the bricfest, a thing I never fail to appreciate, for I am no stranger to red tape which seems to thrive in some countries where authorities are so wrapped up in it that they hardly know whether they are coming or going. The proverbial Spanish good manners are also a welcome change from the general indifferent behavior of most officials in big commercial ports. A Spaniard is a gentleman, however humble his birth.

"Let's go and buy some fish," Bep suggested that first morning at Ciutadella, and I knew what he was going to say the moment he opened his mouth. Bep, an avid fisherman, was forever trailing all kind of hooks over the stern. The three fish he had caught in the past two months hardly satisfied his ambitions. As if trying to compensate for his frustration, he invariably made the fish market his first target in a new port. He would then spend the rest of the morning concocting his favorite dish: fish soup. In all justice, I must say that his dishes were always tasty and nourishing. The one we had that day was no exception. I dislike cooking myself, but I definitely do not object if my crew likes to indulge in such healthy pastimes.

Ciutadella provided more attractions than Fornells. An

ancient city, a former capital of the island, it has a shopping center under medieval arcades in the old part of the town. Many fine palaces of noble Minorcan families still stand, although the weathered walls and closed window shutters gave them a note of melancholy. Their days of glory are gone, never to return.

Our arrival in this quiet town became a minor sensation. Quite a few yachts come during the summer, but winter is hardly time for cruising, and only the inter-island steamer and some cargo schooners enter the strange narrow harbor.

We never failed to attract a crowd. The good citizens thought nothing of stopping dead in the middle of the street to stare at us in amazement. Mark with his blond hair, leather jacket and red and white woolen cap was always the center of attention. He is a handsome boy, and the ladies of the town, young and old, did not hide their admiration for the young sailor. One day we walked along the road to the harbor entrance to watch the arrival of the mail boat. Docking is not an easy matter and can be done only in fine weather. The ship comes in slowly, drops an anchor and then by an ingenious use of cables is turned around and moored to a short concrete jetty, bow facing the entrance.

The intricate maneuver was done quietly and without much fuss under the competent eye of our newly found friend Francisco Mir, Paco to his friends, the harbor pilot who also carried out the functions of French Consular Agent at Ciutadella. He very strangely insisted that we should simply stay the whole winter and move on in spring. We did not disclose that we were bound across the Atlantic, but he suspected as much, for we often discussed with him the Canary Islands, also a Spanish possession, off the coast of Africa. He was full of interesting stories of yachts and ships and knew well Dr. Alain Bombard whom I had met in Tunis. Bombard had made history by crossing the Atlantic in a rubber dinghy without any food on board to prove that a man could survive by drinking seawater and eating plankton. He also wanted to show that this type of craft is a much better life saving device then the conventional lifeboat. On his way from Monte Carlo, Bombard had stayed a month in Ciutadella.

Guided by Paco, we made several most interesting visits to what were the town's two major industries: shoemaking and ornamental jewelry. Minorca is a large exporter of shoes, which are sold in Paris, London and New York. We viewed all stages of production, and it was strange to think that the finished article, to be had here at the factory for the equivalent of five dollars, would be sold in New York for thirty to forty dollars. A considerable proportion of the total output is made by independent artisans working at home. When walking in the narrow street one can see right through open doors which often open to another street and entire families working late into the night.

Right across our berth were several cafes, or rather bars or combinations of both. Paco introduced us to Don Diego café. It became our favorite, and when the time came to give a farewell party, our choice obviously fell on that one. It was a spaghetti lunch for which we used our last package of Tunisian pasta. Mark and Bep were responsible for all preparations, and the whole affair was a huge success. There was much laughing and joking. The local gin, apparently introduced by the English back in the eighteenth century, added much to the merriment of the company. Bep was in raptures over the excellence of this beverage and ordered a dozen bottles to be sent on board. A prudent man, Bep was. He never failed to think of the future and possible emergencies!

The night before we sailed, I smashed my right thumb in the companion sliding hatch. It blew at once into the size of a small potato. The pain was so intense that the half-dozen sleeping pills I took failed to put me to sleep. I got up in a despondent mood, and all day I could not make up my mind whether to sail or not. Finally we all three agreed that it was time to go, and we cast off with much ado. Paco was there to tow us out with his motorboat as it would not be possible for us to leave under sail. As a rule, I always try to sail early in the morning. One has a full night's sleep behind and the day ahead to make a good offing and settle down on board. But under the circumstances, it was preferable to make a night run toward the coast of Majorca and be there at daybreak. It was only just over twenty miles, but it appeared as two hundred. We still had fresh in our minds the struggle of December.

Paco towed us well out of the harbor and then kept for a while alongside urging us to return. I very nearly gave in, but then taking a firm grip on myself, I waved a final farewell and set course for the Cape.

The night was promising to be bitterly cold. Only the thought that we were on the move again kept me from falling back into my despondent mood.

CHAPTER SEVEN

The fog was dense. Standing on the quay, I could almost hear it running down the rigging. I stepped a few paces to look at my ship. What untold romance there was in her. The feeble shore lights reflected through the mist on the white rigging which stood out against the blackness of the February night. The top mast disappeared mysteriously in the darkness, but not her white-painted deck fitting and dodgers. I never tired of studying the details of my vessel. She lay so still, but she was not lifeless. She was merely resting after the hardships of the past months, gathering strength, for we were to set sail again in two days on the voyage west.

The bells of the Cristo church struck midnight as I stepped on board my silent ship. I stood for a while on the afterdeck, my arms resting on the furled mainsail, unable to break the spell of this eerie night. I was trying to delay the moment of going below to the emptiness of the cabin, a feeling I could not shake off since that day a month ago when Bep and Mark left me and returned to Tunis.

It had been a brilliant cold January afternoon when I said good-bye to Bep and Mark. We shook hands. I walked slowly through the city of Palma to the railway station and made my way back across the island to Porto Cristo on the east coast where *Tethys* lay. The ship seemed empty and sad. I sensed a sorrow that only the departure of close friends and loved ones can evoke. In vain, I tried to put my mind to some work on board. It was no use. I spent the rest of the day gazing seaward, getting used to being alone.

Although Bep's decision to go back was a logical outcome of the delay in our sailing schedule – at that time, according to plan, we should have been five hundred miles west of the Canaries – it caught me unaware and at a moment, when my morale was at the lowest ebb, the day after we got into this beautiful L-shaped harbor of Porto Cristo.

It had taken twenty-two hours to sail the fifty miles from Ciutadella. I despaired that we had not been able to make at least Palma at one stretch. At such rate of port-to-port travel, it would take ages to get to the coast of Spain and Gibraltar. Our nerves were on edge. We had an argument about whether to enter Porto Cristo or go further south. I thought it useless to try to make the extra eight miles in the contrary breeze. Bep wanted to go precisely to our destination. Finally, I had it my way, and we dropped the hook at Porto Cristo. Next day the wind was in the west, and there was no question of leaving. Bep lunched in town with Mark. I stayed on board. I was busy re-stowing provisions when Bep appeared in the companionway and handed me a cigar as if trying to soften the blow of what was to follow.

"You know, I decided to fly back to Tunis," he said quickly. "It will only be for a month or at the most six weeks. I simply have to see what's going on at the farm. My family depends on me to be there."

I felt a squeeze in my stomach as the unpleasant thought of the cruise breaking up came over me, but I could give just one answer. "Well then," I said with as much calm as I could muster, "you are free to go whenever you choose. I shall be very sorry to lose you."

"But I shall join you again," he said promptly, "and for goodness sake, don't rush. I shall not call you a coward if I find you still here when I come back."

"It's early to decide on that. I might stay here for quite a while to outfit," I said, "but I shall try to reach Gibraltar, and you can join me there."

We left it at that for the moment. Bep invited Mark and me for dinner. While he went ashore to order a special meal, I took myself off for a long walk to think the matter over. There was no question of work in the state of mind I was in. I had to give consideration to the serious situation I faced with Bep's departure.

I knew Bep had a valid reason for going back. I could not reproach him for his decision. I was sure I could cope with sailing my boat alone. Single-handing is first and foremost a state of mind. I had fitted out the boat to be sailed comfortably by one man. *Tethys* with her self-steering capabilities was well suited for a lonely sailor, but a long period solo at sea required training. It was only to be as far as Gibraltar, or so I hoped, where I could pick both of them up. With a crew of three, it had taken nearly two and half months to cover four hundred miles. I had another five thousand five hundred to cover. My hope was that the worst weather was astern.

That night at dinner I asked Mark whether he would want to go back to Tunis with Bep for six weeks or so. He was willing but was worrying about me. "Tell me, tell me how are you going to stand watches all alone?" he kept asking anxiously. "Oh, don't worry, I will be all right." I was trying to show as little concern as I could, but there was sadness in my heart. When and where was I going to see my companions again?

Next morning, Bep and Mark left for Palma. I followed a day later to help clear some landing permits. In one more day they were gone. I was alone.

*****

To build up my sagging morale, it was essential that I remain for a longish period in port. For that I had to find a plausible reason. I would not admit that I felt apprehensive at the magnitude of the task ahead. I would have none of that. It was, I reasoned, simply a question of getting used to the idea.

After much reflection, I firmly decided not to move until

February 15. I would employ the month until then to refit my vessel. She was in excellent condition but due for a complete repainting. I also wanted to get some equipment that could improve the ship's efficiency, especially now that I was alone.

A letter went to Captain O.M. Watts in London asking for thirty fathoms of nylon cable to replace the throat halyards. With Bep, I had experienced some difficulty in getting the mainsail in, for the manila halyards were not running easily enough through the blocks in spite of their large size. Moreover, they stretched and shrunk considerably, and it was necessary to make frequent adjustments. I had to eliminate that. I had long contemplated the purchase of a direction finder. This was the right moment. I decided to get the Heron DF to go on my Homer receiver and the Sestrel hand-bearing compass. I would make good use of this splendid instrument later on. Another most important item was a windproof kerosene lamp. I had failed to find one at Malta, and there was no time to get one from London before we sailed. Now single-handed, it was essential to have an efficient all-around white running light to warn the large ships. It would be especially important on the run to Gibraltar. I also asked for a sea anchor and two forty-fathom manila coils. The latter items I was to pick up at Gibraltar, as the air freight would have been much too expensive to get them to the island.

The weather the first few days of my stay in Porto Cristo was warm and sunny and quite nice to do the various painting jobs. I gave a coat to the topside and all fittings on deck. The servings, the protective wrapping of small cord wound tight around the ends of the ropes, received a fresh coat of varnish. I repainted the deck with non-skid paint I still had on board. The watertight cockpit made of tin and splitting at the corners was beautifully repaired by a local shop. All that done, I settled down to await the arrival of my equipment. Porto Cristo, a summer resort, was quiet that winter, but an interesting activity had started soon after our arrival. On our way from Ciutadella, we had spotted a small cargo ship driven ashore, which we judged must have occurred quite recently. We could not approach, for the wind was light, and I was afraid of getting stuck near the rocks. Then with Mark's and Bep's departure, there was time to take a closer look at her.

*****

On coming back from Palma after seeing my crew off, I met Cornelius Colthoff, salvage officer of the famous Smith Towing Co. of Rotterdam, Holland. I at once invited him on board, and he in turn promised to take me to the *Rubicon,* the five-hundred-foot Dutch ship on the rocks, which he had come to investigate. I also met Captain Gerri Spyker, master of the *Rubicon,* a young man of thirty; his wife, who traveled with him and was signed on as stewardess; and Chief Engineer Dick Kuyl, who was twenty-four. On board *Tethys,* over a glass of Bep's Minorcan gin, Spyker told me the story of his mishap. I cite it here, for it is a typical example how an error in navigation when coasting can result in the loss of a ship even in perfectly good weather.

The *Rubicon* was bound for the Italian port of Savona with seven hundred tons of scrap iron. After rounding the cape, the skipper chose to sail through the pass between Majorca and Minorca. The route is safe, well marked and free of danger. That is, if you keep at a decent distance from the coast. Captain Spyker, after many years in coastal trade, was apparently fond of cutting his corners rather fine. That night when he came on watch at 6 p.m. GMT it was dark, and the coast to port showing no lights was hardly visible. According to the mate's four-point bearing taken off Porto Cristo light, the *Rubicon* was to pass a mile off the headland. That seemed a bit too close, even to Captain Spyker, so he ordered a five-degree change of course to starboard. Ten minutes later she struck the rocks less than a cable offshore, ripping a huge hole in her bottom, which flooded her forepeak and main cargo compartments. She heeled to starboard, and there she stayed. The crew took to the boats and made for Porto Cristo.

In my opinion, the inaccurate four-point bearing and the fact that she was sailing unnecessarily close to the shore were responsible for the disaster, but I refrained from all comments. I promised myself to be doubly careful on my trip to Gibraltar, half of which was along the southern coast of Spain. Even so, I would miss by a narrow margin putting *Tethys* ashore on Cape Palos!

The day I spent on board the *Rubicon* was full of interest. *Maas,* the company's tugboat mastered by Captain Van der Ende, arrived early in the morning from Malta where she kept station. We went on board, and Colthoff conferred for a long while with the skipper. It was all double Dutch to me, but now and again they would break into English to put me in the picture of what was happening. I learned that the *Maas* on her way from Malta had gone through a violent mistral, and the mate had a list of damage a foot long. The tug was new and beautifully kept as all Dutch ships are. Her crew of twenty was young and efficient. These were men to whom seafaring was a way of life, and no one could match them in this intricate business of marine salvage and towing.

Marine salvage is usually operated on the "no cure no pay basis." The company bears all risks of the operation, so I was not surprised when later that day Colthoff announced he would abandon the wreck. *Rubicon* was full of holes, her scrap iron cargo was completely submerged, and the available pumps could not lower the water in the hold. It would have taken a considerable amount of money and time to get her off, and the first bad weather could break her in two. For a large company like Smith Towing, this was a minor piece of business really not worth the gain. It was therefore abandoned, and the Spaniards took over. They worked hard for two solid weeks and finally brought her to Porto Cristo where she was settled on the sandy bottom. It was most definitely a stroke of good luck, for next day the weather broke, and it blew for many days. Had she remained one more day, there would have been a total loss. I was glad to see her saved, for she was a pretty ship and could have many years of useful life ahead of her.

Human nature is such that we are seldom content with

existing conditions, and when the weather continued fair, I began to feel restless. In a way it was a good sign. I was not altogether displeased with the mounting urge to go to sea again. Without this pressure, no long-distance voyage in a small craft is possible. I spent many evenings walking along the beaches and below in the cabin pondering the reasons and motives that push people to sail the seven seas in small craft. I was trying to analyze my own motives, but I felt it was yet too early to define the force that started me on this voyage. Many months later, in the Atlantic, I was to come as near to understanding as I ever would.

I was, however, committed to wait for the equipment from London and could only wish that the weather would favor me when the time to weigh anchor arrived. Meanwhile, I tried to make the best use of the time given to me. I spent long hours reading sailing directions and studying the charts. I listened nightly to news from Tunis, which came in clear and strong on the Homer receiver. I also listened regularly to news from England, France and Spain, and my knowledge of languages proved most useful. I was well informed on what was happening in the world. It was fascinating to compare the different countries' different interpretations of the same events.

The nights were cold. Sometimes there was frost on deck at seven a.m. when I began my daily chores. I never wore shoes on deck, an excellent way of waking up. It took me about an hour to wash the deck and clean the cabin. Then it was time to make the colors. I observed a strict flag etiquette, for *Tethys* was the first Tunisian vessel in these waters. It was important to make a good impression. I prepared an ample breakfast and enjoyed it at leisure, listening to music. At ten a.m. the sun was high enough to give some warmth, so I would open all hatches and throw the blankets on deck. The sails would be hoisted for drying. Then I would be off for shopping and a stop at the post office.

On Saturdays and Sundays busloads of tourists arrived from Palma. Invariably there was a large crowd filming and photographing my boat. It was most amusing to listen to the comments. Nine people out of ten would take the Tunisian flag for Turkish. I took great pleasure in politely correcting the error. When traveling in a small boat, it is important to exercise the legs at every opportunity. I took good care to walk and run for at least two hours each day, including long afternoon walks around Porto Cristo. I also had springs on board, and I exercised regularly in port. At sea, of course, it was not possible but also unnecessary.

I had little contact with the local population. As is often so with islanders, they were not easy to penetrate. Moreover, I was not in a very expansive mood. I preferred to stay by myself. Now and again, I received a casual acquaintance on board, but only those who were genuinely interested in ships and deep-sea voyaging under sail.

PART TWO

Setting Sail Alone:
Crossing the Atlantic

CHAPTER EIGHT

February 15 was drawing near, and there was still no reply from London about my equipment. I was getting apprehensive lest something had happened to the parcel that was supposed to arrive by air freight. But then on the 14th, a cable came from London giving the flight number and date. A quick telephone call to the British European Airways office in Palma confirmed that my precious freight was at the airport's customs office awaiting collection. I moved at once to anchor in the middle of the harbor and went about preparations for sailing next day, a Sunday.

It was sunny and warm as I moved out of Porto Cristo towed by my friend Pepe, a fisherman from Ibiza. The sea at the entrance was choppy. Without his assistance I would have had great trouble in getting out. *Tethys* handles extremely well under sail, but in narrow waters with a headwind and a confusing sea, a long-keeled boat like her is slow in stays, and to miss going about could be fatal. Once free of the high rocky shore, *Tethys* picked up her skirts. I hastily cast off the towline, for Pepe's little craft had suddenly become the towed boat as my ship jumped ahead under a sudden gust.

The day was perfect, and my spirits rose to a long- unknown height. I had successfully weathered a difficult period. I was at sea once more. *Tethys* rolled easily to the light swell and kept running before the fair wind at five knots. How easy progress is when the wind is fair. I felt elated. A day like that repays you for all troubles and disappointments. I even forgot for a moment that I was alone, that there was no one to share this happy day with me. Steering was so easy that I could well break the rule and read at the helm. I had met Violet some years previously when he was cruising alone in the Mediterranean in his twenty-foot yawl *Nova Espero*. A veteran of two Atlantic crossings, he had sailed in her with Stanley Smith from London via the Azores and Nova Scotia to New York in eighty days. A year previously, the two Smith brothers had brought her across the North Atlantic from Canada to England in forty-six days. When I met Charles in San Remo, Italy, he was on his way back to England after almost a year in the Mediterranean. I was then preparing a long-distance cruise, which ended in total failure.

I liked his honest writing and the description of places I knew so well. The chapter in which he wrote about our meeting was one of my favorites. I admired greatly this slight gentle man who could stand up to the toughest experience at sea in spite of the handicap of a stiff leg. He came again to the Mediterranean on a second lonely voyage in the *Nova Espero,* and then I heard no more from him until many years later, I read he was selling his share in the *Nova.* Apparently he was giving up long-distance voyaging, not at all surprising, for life at sea cannot be maintained. It is a passing state. Sooner or later one has to give it up to return to more conventional life ashore. Few are those who have made it a way of life and succeeded in keeping it up.

I had lost myself in these reflections. The time passed quickly as it always does when one is a in a happy state of mind. Months later in the Atlantic, I was to devote many a day to meditation on the philosophy of small boat voyaging. That afternoon in the Mediterranean, for the first time on this voyage, I had the leisure and conditions conducive to serious thinking about the reasons that led me to set sail. For years I took this urge for sea travel under sail as a natural thing which had lived in me since my beginning. It was there, and it had to be satisfied. Now I was intrigued with what made me long for the far-off seas. What drove me to seek the unknown beyond the distant horizons? What was I hoping to find? Was there to be an answer?

My pensive mood was interrupted by the light tower coming into view from under the squared-off mainsail. I applied myself to the task of taking a four-point bearing to check the distance offshore. Soon the light came abeam. It was time to jibe the ship and head for Palma inside the bay still thirty miles distant. The sun was setting, the sea under the lee of the island was incredibly still, yet I was traveling five knots with the boat so steady that I had the impression it was the land which moved past me. Five miles to the south was Cabrera Island beautifully cut in the evening sky. All was peace and quiet, not a sound came from the land. I heard the gentle ripple of the bow wave and the murmur of the wind.

With the wind abeam, *Tethys* took care of herself. I sat forward on the pulpit for a long while unable to take my eyes off the perfect curve of the sails. It was a moment of great beauty. I felt at peace with the world and myself.

Sunset and the evening chill drove me to the warmth of my cozy cabin where I stretched on the short settee, my legs against the companion steps. Through the open hatch I saw the first stars on the inky blue sky. I could tell at once if *Tethys* deviated from her course, and I dozed off to rest, for entering harbor is always a strain, especially at night.

I made good speed. It was ridiculously easy to sail under such conditions, needing no effort at all on my part. One more fix at ten p.m. and I had Palma ahead. I was abreast of the entrance at midnight, just twelve hours from Porto Cristo and fifty miles made good. Then the irony of it taking me three hours to reach my berth at the Club Nautico's outer pier. The wind had died, there was a strong outgoing current, and I had to row her in. Standing in the cockpit, I worked the long sweeps with strong strokes making only a little headway. At moments like that I began to understand the utility of an engine. Even an outboard, noisy beast as it is, would have been welcome that night. At three a.m. I was finally anchored with my faithful Danforth, stern to quay. I piled into my bunk with a deep sigh of contentment. This time I had made a good start.

Twenty-eight hours later, on Tuesday, February 17, I departed Palma for Gibraltar. This time there was no turning back, the circumstances were all in my favor, and it was up to me to complete the Mediterranean passage in proper style.

It was seven a.m. when I weighed anchor. The air was crystal clear and cold, the sea and sky were the color blue only the Mediterranean knows how to produce.

I brought out my charts and instruments into the cockpit, a practice I was to follow from then on in good weather. After streaming the log off the breakwater, I settled down comfortably at the helm. In such perfect weather the five-hundred-mile passage ahead did not appear of any particular importance. Even the fact that it was my first long single-handed effort did not impress me too much. I felt a supreme confidence in my ability to deal with whatever emergency might arise. To be sure, I was careful not to take any undue risks, and my ship was magnificently adapted for single-handing. I was in perfect physical condition. My morale was high. I was especially pleased with my successful call at Palma. How much one can accomplish in just one day if things go right!

*****

Nine a.m. on Monday after my arrival from Porto Cristo found me pacing impatiently in front of the British European Airways office in the modern part of Palma. I had slept only three hours, but my excitement was so great that I hardly felt any fatigue at all. I was not familiar with Spanish customs procedures and had to reckon with last-minute complications. All I knew was that ships are allowed to import equipment duty free in transit. The office was a full ten minutes late in opening, but I managed somehow to control my temper. When the office manager offered me the services of his assistant to help with the formalities, I was back to normal.

Unfortunately we kicked off on the wrong trail, and it took the best part of the day to get my equipment. Someone had said we should first of all go to an agent who should handle the whole thing. We found the man and were informed that we did not need to employ him, for the parcel was under a certain weight. However, as the items were destined for a ship, we should obtain a certificate from a marine office, the address of which he mentioned, saying that indeed these items were necessary for the ship. We hopped a cab and went off to the said office. After much searching there for someone who could issue such a certificate, we were told that the matter really belonged to a third office. Off we went in a taxi again. Yes, we were told in the new place, it could be given, but the official was not there. He came finally but did not want to sign. From office to office we went pleading and asking. Then someone with more sense and better knowledge of regulations, or perhaps with the good idea of getting rid of us, suggested that all we needed do is ride out to the airport and collect the bloody stuff! Another cab ride, and indeed it was all we needed to do. The customs man in charge was most polite, had the items checked against the invoice, ordered an officer to ride with us to my boat, and we were off. It had taken exactly six minutes.

I spent the afternoon receiving the new halyards. I had never before spliced a nylon cable, and it was quite difficult to handle. But how easily the mainsail could be taken in now! And my lamp! It was a perfect beauty. I stood in the cockpit and simply could not take my eyes off the shiny copper. It had a windproof glass cone inside and was perfectly built and shaped. I could hardly wait to try it out the first night at sea.

I had the best intentions to turn in early that night to be fresh for a first light takeoff the next day, but toward six in the evening when returning on board with some fresh provisions an elderly gentleman whom I rightly guessed to be American, wished me a polite good evening and inquired whether I had a boat in the harbor. We were then at the entrance to the club. I was in such a happy frame of mind that I instantly invited him on board where we prepared to talk and taste some of the rum I had discovered in the after locker, which apparently Bep had stowed away for future reference. My guest was of the opinion that one good glass deserves another. The result was dinner ashore liberally washed down with all kinds of refreshments. It was past midnight before I was back on board. Then I could not resist playing for a couple of hours with my wonderful new gadget, the Heron direction finder. I was up an hour before dawn and weighed anchor soon after.

Sipping my sixth cup of coffee in the cockpit that first day out, I chuckled at the recollection of the previous night's table conversation. On board *Tethys*, we had had quite a few long drinks. I told my guest some of my adventures during the war and in the years that followed. At the end of the dinner he said, "You know, I have been in the Intelligence Service during the war, and I can tell you exactly what you have been doing the last twenty years," and he proceeded to repeat all I had told him a few hours previously on board. He had an excellent memory. I had to grant him that!

All that day I kept in a happy frame of mind. I was on the move again. This time my chances of getting to Gibraltar were good. The only dark spot on a perfect beginning was that my crew was no longer with me. In spite of having been alone for over a month, I was nostalgic for the days when Bep and Mark were with me. I could no longer share my experiences with anyone. To compensate, there was a certain relief in the thought that now I had but one life to answer for: my own. The responsibility for my son and my friend was off my shoulders. It was a strange sensation and one I was not quite certain I was happy to have. A perfect and permanent state of bliss does not exist. Only by a carefully calculated compromise can one approach what usually is called happiness. To me, having a difficult goal to work for is one of the essential conditions to happiness. At this moment I had just that. I felt proud of having successfully weathered three severe storms, although I humbly admitted that without Bep and Mark I would have very likely broken down morally.

I was able, as always when putting to sea, to shut my mind to the many problems I left behind and others I would have to face on the completion of my voyage. The latter was fortunately many months away, really too far off in time and distance to bother me or disturb the feeling of satisfaction I was experiencing at the beginning of this passage to Gibraltar. I was full of strong determination to live to the utmost my adventure and then try to share it with those who would never be able to experience what is, I think, the greatest gift life can give to any man: freedom. A deep-sea voyage in one's own sailing vessel gives the physical experience of freedom, which can only be compared with the physical expression of love. In both cases a man feels on top of the world.

Time goes by quickly when you sail your vessel and have ample food for thought, as I had. The long hours at the helm were reeling off without trouble. I felt no fatigue or boredom the first day out. I knew it was too early to understand, or even try to understand my motives for undertaking such a long voyage, but I could not help thinking of it constantly. I was determined to find out what pushed me to exchange the comfortable and conventional life for an existence basically foreign to a human being. Undoubtedly, life at sea is foreign to men who were born to lead a life on land in the company of fellow humans. Now I was at sea and alone. I could count on myself only, and possibly in Providence, who so far had shown such a remarkable interest in my little boat and her crew. But this was, perhaps, because Mark had been with us and his life was spared and ours too because of him. Now I could not tell whether I was destined to meet my end. I was aware of one thing. I had to go on regardless of what would happen, regardless of consequences. There was but one way. It lay ahead westward. There was no turning back. I had reached the point of no return, of that I was firmly convinced.

The beautiful sunny day gave way to a peaceful evening. I lit my kerosene light and handed in the main. At ten p.m. I turned in, leaving my boat to run slowly to the west.

The following few days were quiet and uneventful. The

weather was good with clear skies and gentle winds, which eventually died away when I was well past the island of Ibiza, the westernmost of the Balearic group. I passed to the north of the island thirty miles from the position where we were caught by the great gale more than two months previously. My Ibiza chart remained clean with one course only drawn upon the spotless surface, how different from our Algerian coast charts where there was hardly any place left for fixes and courses.

On the third day I sighted Spain, and I felt amply rewarded for the many hard months which lay astern. The wind died. The sea became calm and blue. I lay on deck during the warmer part of the day thinking of the delights of deep-sea voyaging. I slept well at nights, coming on deck every two or three hours to look for signs of wind. The Spanish coast was on my starboard ten miles away, visible in the clear air. Now and again I would drift across great patches of muddy water littered with pieces of wood, branches and once even a child's toy, a sad remembrance of the torrential rains and great winds which hit this coast in December.

The days went by as I drifted slowly toward the Cape Palos. I felt no particular urge for speed or contact with land or people. I was settling down to the life on board alone. I was becoming a single-hander. Shore problems were fading away. I was growing attuned to the dangers and problems of the sea. My whole system was undergoing a change, mental and physical. It was a foretaste of my state of mind and body in the Atlantic, and I knew that I could take it. I knew that I was mentally prepared for the test. I was to go through a crisis a few days later off Almeria, but it was to be the last at this time. Not until many months later, nearing the shores of America, was I to experience the mental anxiety which a single-hander is confronted with during long periods of solitude at sea.

Sailing a sea as temperamental as the Mediterranean, in an engineless boat, can only be done by sporadic jumps. Hardly ever is it possible to count on a constant wind and predict the arrival at your destination with any degree of accuracy. In fact, I think the best type of vessel for this inland sea is a motor sailor capable of a good turn of speed under power with a sound sail area to take care of the strong, fair winds. When a breeze began to build up from the east on the fourth day of the calm, my eighth day out of Palma, my heart rejoiced. The predawn hour was very dark but Cape Palos, a quarter of a mile on my starboard beam, stood clear, its powerful light sweeping across the water and over my ship. A lighthouse at close range keeps me spellbound beyond all imagination. Palos is one of the great capes of the Mediterranean, and its light marks the turning point for all who head towards the Straits of Gibraltar from the northwestern basin of the Mediterranean or the Balearic Islands.

I had several restful nights behind me, so the prospect of even a twenty-four-hour trick at the helm was but a pleasant anticipation. I still had some two hundred fifty miles to go, with a fair wind, a sail of about three days for a boat of *Tethys'* size. I hardly dared to hope for the easterly to last that long. The immediate tactics dictated to make the most of it while it lasted.

Steering before the wind in a fore-and-aft rigging sailing boat is tiring, even in a perfect runner like the little *Tethys*. The vessel requires constant attention. The helmsman cannot leave the helm or even relax, for the risk of jibbing is great. A single-hander is simply pinned down to the helm. Later, in the Atlantic, I followed the simple technique of lowering the mainsail for the night, letting the ship run under headsails only. In the Mediterranean where the coast is seldom far, this is not possible. Besides, one simply cannot afford to waste a fair wind. I therefore ran for all my ship and I were worth. The first few hours of downwind sailing are fun. After a day one is tired and boredom sets in. When night comes one positively feels weary, and only the thought of good progress cheers you up.

The wind settled down to a steady force of five on the Beaufort scale, a fresh breeze. I was cutting across the Gulf of Cartagena with the Cape of Gata light as my next checkpoint. I ran all day and the following night, ticking off hour by hour the miles recorded by the patent log.

The Gulf of Almeria opened up early next morning. A slight rain obscured the land now quite near on my starboard bow. The waters around me were dotted with passing ships. I counted fourteen in two hours. They were of many flags, shapes and sizes, all busy on their lawful pursuits, all enjoying the freedom of the boundless sea.

Already there were signs of the breeze wanting to phase out. The steady wind began to lose its strength. It hesitated once or twice, picked up again, blew for a moment, and then cut as if switched off by some invisible hand. I never saw it again for forty-eight hours – miserable, depressing, heartbreaking and discouraging lost hours.

The lightly overcast sky filtered the late winter sun, and it became hot and rather pleasant. I dozed on deck the rest of the morning and the best part of the afternoon. Days were still short at this time of year.

Point Sabinal, an unattractive flat headland of Andalusia, kept me company. From where I lay on the foredeck, I could see its colorless beach, silent witness to the recent tragic loss of the English yacht *Eldothea*. She was battered to pieces in the great gale of December 22, which *Tethys* weathered at anchor in Fornells.

The falling darkness brought no sign of wind. *Tethys* drifted aimlessly in the light current. It was disheartening to see her point to the west. I spent hours trying to keep her headed in the right direction, a futile occupation, for there was not a breath of wind. Months later in the Atlantic when a four-day calm beset me, I was glad of it. But now it was maddening. Fresh in my mind were the endless days we spent on the coast of Algeria at the outset of the voyage.

This time there was no one with whom I could share worries, no one to consult, no one to offer advice, no one to talk to, not even anyone to argue with. When the second night came, and the miserable headland was still there, I felt low. I remained on deck through the night trying to gain some distance, taking shelter only in the heavy downpours which blotted out the seascape every few hours, making the black night still darker.

A foolish thing it was to stay awake all night. I should have known better than to waste my strength in a useless struggle. I had not yet learned the secret of taking advantage of such conditions to accumulate sleep and build up a reserve of stamina which is a prime requisite in this exciting game of voyaging long distance in a small yacht without auxiliary power.

As the night wore on, grave doubts assailed me as to my powers to withstand the rigors of solitude. I asked myself again and again whether I had the mental vigor, moral stability and courage to carry out a task which, difficult in itself, is rendered still harder by the strangeness of isolation. An average inhabitant of a large city as New York, who in the course of his existence is never but a few yards away from thousands of other human beings, will find it hard to fully comprehend the problems of being alone at sea. There are, nevertheless, advantages which cannot be denied. You have but nature to contend with, a nature which is impersonal and quite indifferent about her opponent. There is no one to trip you, no one waiting around the corner to assail you and pick your pocket. There is no one above you to hold you down, no one below you eager to step in your shoes at the first opportunity. Jealousy, hatred, gossip, abuse, the countless crimes of which man only is capable, are absent. Cleanliness of life and singleness of purpose reign supreme at sea.

The third day of calm came and with it hope for a fair breeze. By midmorning a swell set in from the east, a sure indication of wind from that direction. The sky continued overcast, also a sign of an easterly. I tried to keep busy with chores below and on deck, glancing eastward hopefully, ready for instant action. The light lunch, which I usually eat at sea, was followed by a spell below resting. Listening to the weather forecast and some music, I lay in my bunk speculating on my chances of arriving in Gibraltar by the first of March. It was February 27, and I had but one hundred fifty miles to go, not a great distance, but who could tell whether it would take two or three weeks to negotiate if the wind veered to the west? In that part of the Mediterranean with land north and south, the wind blows either from the Atlantic into the Mediterranean or vice versa. Northerly or southerly winds are extremely rare, practically nonexistent. There also is a current setting east, which does not help a westbound sailing vessel. I was stuck in one of the most difficult spots on the whole Mediterranean, and only a good Levanter, the east wind, could solve my problem.

Early in the afternoon there were definite signs of a fair wind. Apparently Providence had decided that I had been tested enough, that I deserved a respite. Finally the wind came, and with it a delightful surprise.

Meeting another ship at sea is always pleasant, but the encounter of two sailing vessels has no equal in excitement. As in most such cases, it took me completely by surprise. One moment the horizon was empty, the next a schooner was bearing on me, distant not more than a mile. She was black, high-sided, under short canvas and obviously making good use of her auxiliary power, for there still was hardly enough wind to keep her canvas steady. She rolled easily to the following swells, intending, it seemed to me, to pass on my starboard some distance away. I would have none of it. I never have tried to stop or signal a merchant vessel, but here was another yacht heading the same way I was. I simply could not resist the temptation of making contact. I was in need of a lift after my two days of depression. She was the answer to my prayers – contact with people – and she was also bringing wind!

I sheeted in all sail to cut across the schooner's bow. I hoisted all flags. I made frantic gestures trying to attract attention. I rushed below for the camera. She was coming my way. Soon I could recognize her features: clipper bow, stern cabin, central cockpit, a staysail schooner with a yard across her foremast, unmistakably a William Garden design. Her hull was dark blue with gray and white. Then I remembered: she was the *Mystic* from Chicago. I had seen her on my visit there in 1957. By this time I was within hailing distance. Introductions and questions shot across the water. We came quite close. She had a crew of five: Chad Baertschy, the owner, and his wife Helen; Musch and Max Rommler of Germany; and Edward Weber from Union City, New Jersey. Meanwhile, she had set the square sail, for the first time since it was made in France, the owner told me. All the time while we were talking and she was sailing on my starboard, I was taking photos (which appeared months later on the cover of the American magazine The Rudder), leaning over the boom gallows, steering with my foot. The wind had picked up, and by then we were sailing smartly. *Mystic* was bound for Gibraltar and then across back to the States via the Caribbean. We agreed to meet again in Gibraltar.

It was getting dark. *Mystic*, a much bigger and faster vessel, began to draw away. The wind had strengthened, but I kept all sail on determined to make the most of it. I had already been ten days out of Palma de Majorca and I was tired and anxious to get to Gibraltar.

I dressed warmly and prepared some food and coffee for an all-night session at the helm. It was not a pleasant prospect, for I already had a sleepless night behind me. I kept ten miles offshore steering due west. I drove her hard all through the long February night. But the thought of the great progress kept my morale high.

Dawn at last, the best time of day on board. I felt a little tired. It was difficult to perform my morning chores, for I couldn't leave the helm for more than a minute or two. I just did the minimum. Then the sun rose, and I stretched like a cat trying to capture whatever warmth there was in the pale glow.

The visibility was good. I could see on my starboard side the coast of Spain stretching right ahead and then curving to the southwest. The sea kept moderate. I ran dead before the wind, riding with the bigger seas, a wonderful sensation. I tried to identify the coast. By Jove, if it was not Gibraltar right ahead, distant some twenty-five miles.

I usually keep a careful dead reckoning, and this prompt appearance of the famous rock somehow did not quite agree with my calculations. But then the log usually under-registers when running. I sailed all morning. By two p.m. I positively identified Gibraltar. I rushed down below to change my clothing and put some order in the cabin. I cleaned the decks and made everything shipshape and Bristol fashion, as the saying goes.

I am rather proud of my ship. I like her to look her best at all times and especially when making port. Ah, there was Europe Point, another hour to go. I was a little surprised to see the concrete slopes on the eastern side which collected water. I ran on, but the wind was falling. Europe Point hardly seemed to be getting nearer. Another hour went by. I became uneasy. But the easterly current is strong, I thought, so I went on.

It was strangely unfamiliar this Gibraltar. I knew the approach from a previous trip in a steamer. This somehow did not quite agree with what I remembered. That was so many years ago, so I went on. I was now not more than two miles off, ready for the bay of Gibraltar to start opening up. It was strangely quiet. One small Spanish steamer only was coming towards me. I looked to the south and was startled not to see Africa, but it often is hidden in a thick haze. I went on anxious and uneasy, another half-mile to go. I was almost there.

Suddenly my heart nearly leaped out of my mouth. There was no bay all around the point. The coastline continued westward and slightly to the north. There was nothing straight ahead of me, nothing to the south. I panicked. I had missed Gibraltar. I was being carried into the Atlantic! I was lost. I simply did not know my position. It seemed so stupid to get lost on a one hundred thirty mile passage. Incredible.

I sat in the cockpit incredulous and distressed. I tried to collect my scattered thoughts. I was overtired, and it was a clear case of hallucination. It was not Gibraltar at all. But if it was not Gibraltar, what was it? I did not know.

I hove to at once and went below all shaken. I rested for twenty minutes, then plotted again my course, starting from the last fix off the fishing port of Adra, which I had passed twenty hours before. Slowly the picture cleared itself. I was off the Calaburras Light, a full forty miles from Gibraltar. I sighed with relief, but the thought that I had been a victim of so strong a hallucination troubled me greatly, for I feared that it might repeat itself in the future with a less happy ending.

The wind fell light. I was again faced with an all-night trick at the helm. I had no choice but to go on. So I just sat there trying hard not to fall asleep. Just after one a.m. I sighted the light of Gibraltar. A great moment this. At last I was nearing the end of my Mediterranean passage. Four long months had gone since I left Tunisia with a crew of two. Now I was reaching Gibraltar alone.

The east current was against me. From there on, I had to be careful and try to find the best course not to be carried back to where I came from. I was so excited that the wariness I felt in the early part of the night, my third full night on deck, vanished like magic.

I organized myself on deck. Light, food, charts, hand-bearing compass were placed within my reach in the cockpit. Every half-hour, I took exact bearings of all visible lights. The wind was fair and strong, but I had the current against me. The best I could do was to point towards Gibraltar steering southwest and make good a southerly course. The tide rips became more frequent and violent as I neared the Rock. My tired brain began to play tricks on me. I defended myself the best I could with countless cups of coffee, sardines and honey. Finally the current began to turn, and I made good speed towards Europe Point. The sight was eerie. There was a low half moon casting a ghastly light through breaks in the heavy clouds. The Rock to the west appeared twice its normal size. The many red and orange lights gave it a weird appearance.

As I came nearer, the Rock took the shape of a huge elephant with its trunk lying flat on the water. I was terribly tired and under great tension. At two a.m. I was a mere ten miles off. The current was turning in my favor. I could steer straight for the Europa Point. I thought I would never reach it. Three a.m., four a.m. – still miles to go. Ten minutes to five. I was almost there. Finally the bearing began to change with great speed. I knew I was not more than half a mile off. At five I rounded Europa

Point and headed north into the bay. It was beautifully calm close under the lee of the Rock. It was still completely dark. Two or three boats fishing with powerful lights seemed like the only living things in this uncanny world.

The wind now came in great gusts down the western slope. I headed straight for the southern entrance. I knew I should have first gone to the anchorage, but I was too tired. I didn't care. All I wanted was shelter and a chance to sleep. I was not to get my sleep till late the following night. I passed the huge breakwater unchallenged and went right in, a thing I should never have done and for which I was duly punished later on by being refused permission to moor my ship in the naval harbor. Powerful gusts of wind were coming from all directions. It was difficult to keep a course. One moment I would be becalmed, the next I would race with the lee deck awash. I chose a suitable moment and got the mainsail off, then jib and staysail, and went on under bare pole looking for some place to drop the hook to await daylight. I could not make a decision and went on and on till I knew I could go no further. Something like a wooden jetty loomed dead ahead, so I let go promptly and swung around head into the wind, stern dangerously close to a rough shoreline, the thing I took to be a jetty. There was no question of going to sleep. I spent the last hour of darkness sitting in the cockpit praying the anchor would hold. Thank God it did.

Soon after seven I noticed some airmen ashore not far off and hailed them to get me a tow. It came quickly. In less than ten minutes the police launch was alongside and took me in tow. Not an easy matter, for it was blowing quite hard. They took me out of the harbor to the end of the Gibraltar airport runway where I was told to anchor. I was cleared without great trouble or red tape. I was even towed into a sheltered spot just under the northwestern side of the Rock.

CHAPTER NINE

It was Sunday, the first of March, cold, gray, depressing and rainy. I made my way through the main street full of bazaars, crowded and busy even on a holiday. I knew Gibraltar well from a previous visit soon after the Second World War. I walked slowly, trying to recapture the atmosphere of the past. I always do that when going back to places I know – and never succeed.

The spacious but somber dining room of the Bristol was crowded. I selected a table in the back from where the whole room and its windows were visible. Being used to the unlimited horizon of the sea, I liked to have as much open space around me as possible. Strangely, the inside of a cabin does not produce any claustrophobic effect.

White-coated waiters circulated with ease among the labyrinth of tables, performing their duties with the skill of many years of practice. I could not help thinking about how boring their occupation seemed, yet perhaps there was security in their lives. Yes, I thought, security, man's craving for security, security of jobs, security in travel, security at home, in the street, in the place of work, national security, international security, security from losing a job and falling sick, old-age security, all kinds of security!

In direct conflict with this modern craze for security, bordering on hysteria, is the desire to live an adventure, the desire to live an exciting and novel experience, the curiosity of the unknown and also fear of it – altogether a confusing but fascinating problem. Has the spirit of adventure been condemned to disappear? Or is it just assuming new form: adventure in science, space exploration, exploration of the human mind and, in time, other fields? Such adventure would be accessible to only a chosen few. All others would have to live their adventures vicariously. I would rather have life direct, tangible, personal – yes, personal – something I could call my own. Something no one could take away from me. Adventure. It was here. I had it. Security? Did I want it? Perhaps.

My train of thought was interrupted by a waiter offering me the menu. I ordered carefully: vegetable soup, roast beef, salad, fresh bread and butter, and beer. I savored to the full the pleasure of the first meal ashore. No need to hurry. It was essential to relax, for although the hard winter was far astern and I had conquered innumerable obstacles, there still were serious problems to be dealt with pertaining to the voyage and also of a private nature.

I was finally on the threshold of the Atlantic. Well, nearly so, for there still was the notoriously difficult Straits of Gibraltar to negotiate. Sailing ships with power can go through it only under the right conditions. There is the permanent easterly current from the Atlantic into the Mediterranean through the center of the straits, on both sides of which the tidal streams rush along the coast of Spain and North Africa, changing in direction every six hours or so. With the wind in the west, it is virtually impossible to gain any ground against the current even with a westgoing tide. The combination of tide and wind must be just right. There is no fixed set of rules that permit one to predict with any accuracy when the weather will be favorable. Most of the time it's a question of waiting in readiness to take off the moment the Levanter starts. In my case, it was nineteen days!

There was, to be sure, an ample reserve of time to cross the Atlantic in good season. Two alternatives are offered to those heading west from Gibraltar with America as their ultimate goal. A fall crossing is favored by those wishing to visit the West Indies and then proceed to New York in the early spring. Or a spring crossing is the way if you wish to arrive in America ahead of the hurricane season which starts in June. Sailing from Gibraltar or Tangier to New York via the trade winds, the distance to run is four thousand six hundred nautical miles, while the direct shortest route between the two points is three thousand two hundred. A ship of my size with a crew of one cannot hope to average more than fifty miles a day on the whole run. One has to reckon, therefore, for the voyage to last up to one hundred days. In 1923, Alain Gerbault made a voyage over the same route in the thirty-nine-foot cutter *Firecrest* in one hundred one days. In 1950, Edward Allcard took eighty days in the thirty-four-foot yawl *Temptress*. My *Tethys*, at only twenty-five feet, was the smallest of this trio, but her sailing qualities were certainly not inferior to those of her two predecessors. I could expect with confidence to cross in eighty to one hundred days

Somehow, that first day ashore, I had a strange feeling that Bep and Mark would not continue with me, that I was destined to go alone. Perhaps I was also conditioning myself to the idea of a lonely voyage. Two days later I had the answers to my cables. Bep regretted, but family and business matters were keeping him at home. Mark was back at school and after the slow and hard trip in the Mediterranean was not too enthusiastic about coming along. I understood. I spent one morning packing the gear of my crew to send back to Tunis. It was a sad occasion, which even the bright rays of the spring sun could not dispel. A chapter in my life was closing with a finality that was hard to accept.

I have since seen many deep-sea voyages abandoned because of the crew breaking up. Most fortunately I was immune to such danger. *Tethys* was a perfect single-hander. I could carry on along wherever I wanted to go. With Mark and Bep on board, it would have been necessary to stop at the Canaries and then somewhere in the West Indies. Alone, I could sail directly to New York by the trade wind route. The trade winds! The balmy nights under the tropical starry skies! The blue seas! The romance of a deep-sea voyage!

Walking along the rainy streets of Gibraltar, I tried to boost my spirits with visions of delights ahead of me. With these in mind, I set eagerly to complete the final preparations for the crossing.

Normally, I would have taken Gibraltar as my port of departure, but my American visa sent out from the Embassy in Tunis was waiting for me at the American Consulate General in Tangier. I had to collect it personally. All my mail was also there. There was no choice but to plan a stop in this ancient Moorish stronghold on the North African coast. It lay thirty miles to the west, across the straits. The thought of seeing Morocco was not unpleasant. It would be interesting to see the changes since my last visit there in 1946. I welcomed the chance to savor once more the exciting, delightful atmosphere of North Africa which I loved so much and which I desired to carry as my last impression of land, rather than to remember the indifference of Gibraltar. A purely personal preference, this.

After the thorough refitting at the Balearics and the twelve-day good weather passage to Gibraltar, *Tethys* was in top condition, needing only the normal maintenance any sailing yacht in commission requires periodically. Her bottom, although not too bad after four months in water, had to be painted again. It is wise to begin a long passage with a clean hull. It adds considerably to the speed and safeguards the wooden planking against attack by worms, although this latter risk is practically nil at sea. I decided to careen her at Tangier where the rise of tide is quite sufficient to clean boats of *Tethys'* size. I concentrated on improving my equipment and taking in stores for a hundred days.

I was most fortunate to meet Captain Undeary, a pilot who also ran a service providing yacht equipment. I spent many hours in his delightful place, choosing carefully the items I needed. I bought a new stout anchor and one hundred fifty feet of manila to carry in addition to the two warps I already had on board. I planned to fix it permanently on the after grating to be prepared to counteract stress when running became hard. I was to have an ample proof of the excellence of this method. Sail twine and needles, yacht marlin, paint and many other items were brought aboard. I also invested some money in charts of the West Indies and Bermuda. There was now on board a full set of charts covering both sides of the Atlantic, including all islands. Strangely enough, for reasons I shall never understand, I did not take the charts of New York and the surrounding coast. Perhaps subconsciously, I still desired to see the exotic Caribbean. Or was I afraid to think of the magnitude of my undertaking, of the direct passage to New York, of endless, lonely days at sea? I am not too sure. In any case, it was a grave oversight. I was to regret bitterly my error months later approaching New York with nothing but a primitive Esso map to guide me into this greatest of all seaports, where a small sailing vessel is more lost than in the emptiness of the mid-Atlantic with nearest land a thousand miles away.

The success of any expedition depends largely on the care given to the preparations. A sea voyage must be particularly well thought out. A sailing vessel must be self-sufficient in all possible ways. Independence from land and outside help is essential to a deep-sea voyager. Attention to detail and foresight are also, in my mind, among the greatest pleasures of long-distance sailing. The excitement, the anticipation of adventure is almost equal to the supreme feeling of independence and the sense of well-being which comes when you finally put to sea. Preparations for a voyage, to me, are an integral part of adventure, and the days spent at Gibraltar following my arrival were full of pleasant activity.

I was embarked upon a lifelong project. There was nothing haphazard about my voyage. All elements essential to adventure were there. For those who are particular about the purpose, who want to know the whys and whatfores, the reason behind, for those who are devoid of all sense of adventure, I had a ready and valid answer: I was traveling to take up residence in my new country. After all, one had to do it one way or another, and mine was just as good as any.

In my endeavor to prepare for the voyage, I left nothing to chance. I do not hesitate to state that *Tethys* was one of the best-prepared little ships for such a voyage. I spared neither time nor money to give her the best of care and the best in gear. My efforts were well rewarded. Apart from losing a sea anchor on the coast of Algeria, I had no accidents in the course of what was to be a six thousand-mile, eight-month voyage. I am rather proud of this.

After a week in port, *Tethys* was ready to sail. I began to fret at the delay caused by the weather. The wind remained persistently in the west, and there was no question of departing. I employed my time the best I could. I read, walked and relaxed. I was a frequent visitor on the schooner *Mystic*. She looked impressively large to me, but she was only forty feet on deck. Secretly I envied the companionship that her crew of five enjoyed. Mine was a solitary journey. Theirs was a common effort. Yet I was to complete the voyage many months ahead of *Mystic*, for she like many others suffered from the ill effects of a broken-up ship's company.

Yachts were few in Gibraltar that spring. *Mystic* and *Tethys* were the only two headed west. There was an interesting yawl of about forty feet, the *Margaret Louise*. I never met her owner, who was away in Europe, but the crew of two, an Englishman and a Dane, were nice fellows, and I enjoyed their company. The yacht was old and of a rather light construction. The owner planned to take her on some sort of expedition, for she was being outfitted with many expensive items. There was a large library on board, diving equipment, guns and a complete set of navigation instruments. Her crew had only a vague idea of her owner's projects. The Red Sea was mentioned on several occasions, and my imagination flared at the thought of this exotic sea. It would be great to go there, but I quickly shook the temptation off. I had my own adventure to attend to.

Also lying at the quay was the powerful forty-seven-foot Colin Archer-designed *Stavanger*, veteran of several Atlantic crossings. Aboard was a Mrs. Nielsen, the wife of Dr. Nielsen, who was lost in December in the wreck of the English yawl *Eldothea* on the coast of Spain. The memory of the great storm still lived in Gibraltar where winds gusted up to one hundred twenty-two knots.

Walking by, I often saw Mrs. Nielsen working on deck. Once or twice I said good morning, intending to open up a conversation but always courage failed me. I simply did not dare to intrude. I felt I was not entitled to break into her private world. I was not yet a member of the exclusive fraternity of those who have crossed oceans in small sailing crafts. My desire to help might be taken for a crude curiosity. No, definitely, I could not approach her. I felt boundless admiration for this courageous woman who, far from cursing the sea, was carrying on the life she had shared with her late husband. I learned from people around the dock that she was awaiting some friends to help her sail the *Stavanger* to Norway, where she intended to go on living aboard with her small son.

As the days went by and there was no sign of a fair wind, I became moody, ill-tempered and impatient. The ship was fully stocked and ready for sea. I could not improve her or add to her seaworthiness. I was already over four months on my way, and there only were seven hundred fifty miles made good to my credit. Ahead there still was an ocean to be dealt with, nearly five thousand miles of it. I knew that I should get started soon. The miserable thirty miles between Tangier and me again loomed large on my horizon. I began to fear that little bit of water. It is the state of mind that keeps one going. It is the happy, confident mood that accomplishes miracles and drives men to go on their chosen road. It was disturbing to think that I might, by a prolonged stay in port, be affected by a loss of faith. It would have been bad to embark on a crossing in anything but a state of perfect peace of mind and mental balance. I thought the problem over, and rather than risk such serious consequences, I decided to swallow my pride and look for a tow.

The matter was not easy. There were, to be sure, many crafts crossing over to Tangier. None as I could see was suitable. My little *Tethys* could never have endured a towing speed of more than seven knots. Nothing puts greater stress on a wooden hull than a speed excessive to her maximum hull speed. Gerbault's *Firecrest* was lost in tow precisely in such circumstances. It would have to be someone willing to steam at five knots or less if the sea got rough. *Mystic* had but a small engine, and willing as Chad Baertschy was, he could not oblige. A yacht would have been the best, so I walked daily along the jetties looking for a likely ship.

One afternoon, it must have been ten days after my arrival, a husky, well-kept converted motor fishing vessel caught my eye. She had a well-shaped deckhouse aft, a cabin coach roof for the best part of her deck and high bulwarks. Apparently, she carried all kind of equipment, for her superstructure was well-adorned with various forms of aerials and gadgets, including a radar. I was impressed and I decided to make contact. She wore, I noticed, the burgees of one of the well-known British services yacht clubs.

She was tied up at the jetty, lying alongside. I stood there patiently waiting for someone to appear on deck, not wishing to intrude. At last, a distinguished looking head emerged in the main companion. I stated my case politely.

"Well, naturally, that could be arranged." The gentleman's voice was smooth, well-bred and obviously American. "But say, why don't you talk with the skipper-owner? I am only chartering the ship."

The captain was not around, so I came back that evening and found him in the deckhouse, which apparently was also his quarters. I again stated my case and asked for help. He was most sympathetic, understood well my problem and was willing to cooperate. "But, my dear chap, I am under charter, you know. You had better ask the charter party, they work for National Geographic magazine." It was clear that areas of responsibility and prerogatives were somewhat mixed up on this good ship!

I at once suggested that we should all meet and discuss the matter. The distinguished looking man was on board, we requested his presence, and I opened up by reference to the famous journal. "I hear you are with the National Geographic, sir," I said.

"Well, not really. We did propose to send them material from our forthcoming trip on the west coast of Africa, but it's nothing definite."

As he did not volunteer any more information, I dropped the subject and went straight to the point. I again requested help in getting across to Tangier. Now both parties were most willing. We studied the charts. It was agreed they would use their own warp, tow at not more than four knots and let me go well inside the Bay of Tangier to save me from a possible sweeping out by the tidal current. It was also settled that I should wait at the end of the Gibraltar airport runway, as it would be more convenient for the yacht to approach me. I was elated and grateful. I offered profuse thanks. Here were people of the sea, I thought. One cannot go wrong in such good company. Real friends, those!

I was to be ready in two days. Next evening I came again to chat with my newfound friends. Only one was on board, a young, well-dressed man with rosy cheeks and a frank face. He sat on the sliding hatch, his feet dangling inside the companionway. I was determined to find out some more about the mysterious errand they were engaged upon.

"I shouldn't really say it, but do you know that the man in charge has the personal rank of an ambassador in the State Department?" he volunteered. It was news to me indeed.

"What's your job?" I asked cautiously, not wanting to appear too eager.

"I am a photographer," he said. "We have a complete photo lab on board. I can even develop color."

From where I stood on deck, the main cabin was clearly visible. One part of it, I noticed, was equipped as an office with typewriters, files and all the odds and ends of bureaucracy.

An ambassador, a photo lab, an office – all that off the west coast of Africa in a motor yacht. A most intriguing combination.

"Tell me, what are you after?" I asked.

111

"I'll be darned if I know." He laughed my question away. Then getting up, he changed the subject, and there was no more reference to their voyage.

That night I moved out to anchor at the end of the runway as agreed. Early in the morning it began to blow from the east. For a time I contemplated a run to Tangier, finally deciding against it. It was unwise to cross in the sea that was probably running in the straits. After all, I had a tow, which would be much safer. It blew hard for several days. The wind went to the west. I pitched violently into the short, choppy sea. For three full days I waited for the motor yacht to come. Finally, in a driving rain, I hailed a passing launch and went inside the harbor. The jetty where she lay was empty, and I was told she had left the day after my last visit on board.

I have her name noted, but very likely I shall never know who the strange people on board were or what was their business – one of the mysteries I shall never solve and a rare instance of discourtesy at sea.

I sailed next morning, March 19. The day was brilliant. A strong easterly was blowing, raising an impressive plume of smoke along the ridge of the Rock. I had tacked two reefs in my main for ease of handling. It was a backbreaking job to get the anchor in. I have no winch of any kind, and I was sick with effort pulling the four tons of my boat towards the hook, against the choppy sea and the strong wind. By nine I was on my way sailing fast.

The ride through the current stream was wild and full of excitement. The strong wind blowing against the current kicked up a nasty steep sea. Any other boat with lesser talents for running than *Tethys* would have had quite a job coping with the seas which seemed to want to pile one upon another. It was a battle of water against the wind. I cut diagonally across the stream, checking my progress all the time with shore bearings. The daily ferryboat from Gibraltar to Tangier was overtaking me to port. A large Italian liner was heading east steady as a rock. In three days she would be home.

Soon I was out of the main current in the smooth waters of the westgoing tide. The Bay of Tangier lay ahead, well visible, the town climbing the hills beyond. I hauled in the main well outside the harbor entrance and ran in under the headsail.

The inner harbor was sheltered and peaceful. I glided in, losing speed gradually in the lee of the buildings. A moment later I let go the hook close to the jetty of the Tangier International Yacht Club.

CHAPTER TEN

The street was crowded on the sunny Friday afternoon of my arrival in Tangier. It was pleasantly cool in the shade of the buildings as I made my way along the steep road towards the center of town. The American Consulate was one of my objectives. The colorful throng around me was friendly. I felt comfort in being able to mix in that multiracial crowd. The familiar smell of North Africa was there: a mixture of charcoal, smoke, spices- and leather. It was strong, satisfying, almost tangible. Smell is an integral part of the scene around me. It gives reality to the picture. It makes you like it or hate it. A traveler, and I consider myself one, is particularly conscious and alive to the sense of smell. Nothing helps better to remember an experience as the recollection of smell. England I best recall by the peculiar, coaly smell of a railway carriage. Sweden to me is more than anything the woody scent of its abodes and countryside alike. Italy's wine-perfumed, stony dark, cellar-like restaurants will always help me to visualize that country. America, too, has a vigorous, young energetic smell of a new world. It can be sensed a hundred miles offshore, no mistake there. On closer acquaintance it breaks into a whole spectrum of sub-smells: the fishy sea winds of Gloucester; the gasoline-saturated atmosphere of New York; the sun-baked, dry, hot, still air of Phoenix; the steamy, oppressive humidity of Washington, D.C. One could go right across the continent. Together it all blends into a harmonious entity.

It was a great moment when in the strange little office of the American Consulate General, I was handed my permanent visa to enter the United States of America, all legalized and properly sealed. Frank Panayotti, the consular official, shook my hand warmly, giving me this key to a new existence. He was the instrument chosen to give a new life to a perfect stranger, little knowing that he himself was already doomed to exit this world so tragically only a few days later.

In my pocket were several letters of introduction to various notables of the city. I was undecided whether to use them or not. Finally I chose not to. The only person I really wanted to meet was Dr. Robert Shea, for many years director of the American School in Tangier. It was too late to see him. So as usually is my want on the occasions when I am alone the first evening ashore, I strolled leisurely towards my favorite place in town, in this case the Menzah Hotel.

Tired from the long walk, I slumped with a sigh of relief into the comfortable settee of the spacious lounge. The pile of mail by my side promised to keep me busy for the rest of the evening. For the moment, I just sat observing idly the various people in my field of vision, pondering the motives which push men to wander across the face of the earth.

The atmosphere of a good hotel has a strangely soothing and restful effect. It is a place of refuge for a weary voyager, a temporary home for those who seek the satisfaction of a journey in quest of that elusive goal, so difficult to grasp –adventure.

*****

The three weeks I spent in Tangier were active and interesting. Bob Shea took me under his wing, and in his company I was able to get an intimate view of this fantastic city, once an international zone, now under the sovereignty of independent Morocco. Bob's knowledge of the country was unique. We spent hours discussing the past, present and future of North Africa. I made myself at home in his apartment, although I always returned on board for the night. His shower, his library, his car, his time were all at my disposal. He spared no effort in trying to make my stay happy and profitable. It was a most gratifying feeling to be looked after by someone who did not expect anything in return. I am always deeply touched by human kindness, by friendship, by generosity. He also gave me the companionship for which I longed.

There was no longer need to keep secret the ultimate goal of my voyage. For the first time I felt entirely free to discuss my projects with people around me. I was astounded to discover the great interest people had in a lonely man setting across an ocean in a small boat. It was not, to be sure, the sailing that captured the imagination. Three other deep-sea yachts were preparing to set off from Tangier. There was the schooner *Mystic,* skippered by an old acquaintance of mine. A charming German couple were bound, they said, for South Africa, in a steel, thirty-five-foot cutter. Another German yacht was a rather badly kept ketch of thirty-four feet. She looked strange and most un-yachtlike. Her ship's company was still stranger. Her skipper was a handsome man of about forty, a former Luftwaffe officer with a wooden leg. His mate was a powerfully built young man, also a German, recently out of the French Foreign Legion. The third member of the crew was a pallid looking but pretty Spanish girl, not more than twenty. I could not help wondering how the captain proposed to solve this triangle. He must have been a navigator of considerable aptitude. I politely but firmly declined the offer to sail in company.

None of these yachts, interesting as they were, appeared to excite the good people of Tangier. All their attention seemed to be centered on *Tethys* and her lonely mariner. I was interviewed on several live and recorded programs in Spanish and French. I was being compared to Alain Gerbault and Dr. Alain Bombard. I felt flattered but a little embarrassed, for I had not yet achieved anything worthy to be ranked with illustrious navigators. There were articles and photos in the local dailies. I had a stream of visitors on board. Everyone was kind to me and helpful. To the

French-speaking peoples, and this language is one the three commonly spoken in Tangier, the term "navigateur solitaire" has an appeal perhaps unequaled in other tongues. It is invariably linked with some romantic reasons for the voyage, an unhappy love affair perhaps? After all, why not let everyone look upon the subject in his own way and see in it whatever the imagination wishes to suggest? This interest was far from unpleasant, for it was one more proof of man's need for adventure even if it had to be lived through the experience of someone else.

*****

The anchorage at the International Yacht Club was most convenient. *Tethys* lay to two anchors to restrict her swinging to the tide which she, a Mediterranean baby, was experiencing for the first time. There was a landing float, and three boatmen assured the service. There was no need to use my little rubber dinghy. The clubhouse was spacious, with wide French windows opening on the waterfront. It was a most satisfying place to relax and watch my ship from. Albert Bendelac, in his capacity of the club's secretary, ran the place efficiently. His courtesy contributed much to make my stay most enjoyable. I was to look upon that last port of call as the best of the whole voyage.

The enjoyment, the success of a project upon which I was engaged depends to a large extent on the ability and opportunity to recuperate both physical and mental strength. Physically, any normal person can, after a period of adaptation, withstand the rigors of a prolonged life at sea. There is no doubt that voyaging in a small vessel is at times most strenuous. The almost constant violent motion, the lack of sleep and physical effort, all these call for considerable stamina. Inevitably, a time comes when your mental powers can no longer cope successfully with the fatigue. You feel overpowered by the magnitude of the task ahead, and although still fit and capable of effort, your morale begins to sag alarmingly and you are only a step from becoming sea weary to the point of seriously considering giving up. It is an extremely dangerous state of mind which at all cost must be avoided. Once reached, there rarely is a way out, short of a very prolonged complete change of surroundings, like taking up poultry farming, for instance.

That past winter, at the Balearics I had been near such a dangerous sea weariness. Although now, at Tangier, I felt healthy both in mind and body, I wanted to make absolutely sure to sail in the best possible shape. I am but a very average human being. I possess none of the exceptional physical strength of Marcel Bardiaux, who in his sloop *Les 4 Vents* made the remarkable eight-year voyage around the world. Nor do I have the fanaticism and perseverance of Alain Gerbault, the great single-hander, or of Jacques Yves Le Toumelin of *Kurun* fame. Absent also in my case is the experience of having gone to sea professionally, like Captain Louis Bernicot whose two-year voyage around the world in *Anahita* will long remain an example of efficiency and success. Thinking of these and other small boat voyagers, I fully realized my shortcomings, but I really saw no valid reason why, with careful preparations, I should not stand a good chance of succeeding. Paramount in importance stood out a healthy mind. Yes, the secret lay in carefully preparing the mind, body and gear. From now on, there would be no more room for failure.

Solitude, although very desirable at times, even necessary, is basically a foreign state to a normal person. I was well aware of the fact that my principal weakness lay in a rather strong need for companionship. And yet there was in me an unexplainable compulsion to sail alone. It would not have been too difficult to find a willing companion, but since the departure of Bep and Mark it never crossed my mind to look for someone else. It was either Bep or Mark or both of them or none at all. I felt this adventure belonged to the three of us. They had shared the most difficult part of it. I was under a moral obligation to carry on alone.

Most fortunately, unlike the other ports of call in the Mediterranean, Tangier gave me human companionship. I decided, therefore, not to hurry my departure but wait for a propitious weather. I had had enough of beating against contrary winds. I felt no inclination to risk a bad start. It was early in the year yet. I could afford to wait and enjoy myself. I was building up reserves of moral strength I could call upon in moments of stress which unavoidably assail a lonely sailor.

The mornings I spent on small jobs on board, correspondence, a little writing. The afternoons I gave to visits in town, walks, a call at the American library, shopping for small items I still needed. The evenings were invariably jolly in company of Bob Shea, Evelyn and Ron Rohner of the American School and many others. Musch and Max Rommler of the *Mystic* were also my close companions.

One afternoon Evelyn took Musch, Max and myself in her car to Cape Spartel, a promontory at the entrance to the Straits of Gibraltar. Standing at the elevated point close to the lighthouse, I had my first glimpse of the mighty Atlantic Ocean. I looked for a long while at this endless expanse of water, fascinated by the brilliant path laid across the surface by the setting sun.

On April 1 *Mystic* sailed for Casablanca, the Canary Islands and across. I felt soon it would be my turn to go. From that day on, the excitement of departure was upon me. The Atlantic, so very long out of my reach, was becoming real at last. Before I left, however, I was to experience something which shook me, and whose significance I do not understand to the present day.

Responding to my invitation, Frank Panayotti came to the club one evening, a huge pile of magazines under his arm. "Something to occupy your mind on your long trip," he said. I thanked him for the thoughtful gesture, and we went to the club's cozy bar for a glass of beer.

We talked for a while of my future in America, and he gave me some details concerning my visa, which he had held for me at the Consulate since December. Then the conversation gradually drifted on to more general subjects of religion, life death, the existence of God. He was visibly troubled by some inner doubts.

"Have you ever thought of the afterlife?" he asked, watching me intently.

"Frequently"

"Do you believe in it?"

"Yes."

"But what is it like?"

"I cannot answer that. No one can. No one knows."

"You are right. You are right. No one has ever come back from there. No one ever will."

We fell silent for a long while. I ordered two more beers.

He turned away staring into the blackness of the night outside. His powerful shoulders seemed to sag a little under the weighty problems. Persistently, he came back to the issue.

"Yes, no one can tell what is on the other side. But we shall all know one day. This is one thing no human being will fail to find out. Whatever our lives here, we shall all go there one day. No one can escape."

We moved outside onto the water's edge.

With a vague gesture, he indicated the dark mirror of the sea.

"Now take, for instance, the belief in resurrection and the final judgment. Supposing a person drowns and his body is eaten by fish and digested. I ask you, what happens then?"

A chill came from over the water. I shuddered with a sudden feeling of apprehension. I said nothing.

"What troubles me most is why God in his infinite goodness makes children suffer. I will never understand that. A grown up man, that can be explained, but a child, innocent defenseless! Why? Why?"

I remained silent, for I could give him no comfort.

"We shall all know one day," were his parting words.

Two days later he had the answer to his problems. He drowned with his ten-year-old daughter while fishing on a windy afternoon off the treacherous Malabata Point.

I sailed a week after.

CHAPTER ELEVEN

Sunday, April 12, was clear and windy. I had announced my intention of sailing at four in the afternoon on the outgoing tide.

I attended an early mass with Bob Shea. The rest of the morning I spent stowing away provisions and securing equipment for the sea. I tried to conceal the intense excitement that permeated each fiber of my brain. The hours dragged with annoying slowness.

At two, some friends came to see me off. We sat in the club's lounge talking and joking. Tension relaxed and disappeared. At twenty minutes to four, I rose and very casually strode to the waiting dinghy manned by one of the club's hands. I hate saying good-byes.

Someone was running down the wooden float. I turned around. "Your sweater, you have forgotten your sweater." Evelyn Rohner, out of breath, was handing me my heavy, white woolen sweater.

In a few moments I was on board and heaving the anchor in. As soon as it broke out of the bottom, the club's launch began to tow me towards the entrance of the inner harbor. I cast off the stops and without hurry began to set the main, then jib and forestaysail. I let go the tow and gathered speed passing ahead of the launch.

The last good wishes came across the widening gap – huge Bob Shea, little Evelyn Rohner, Professor Mercier and his redhead daughter Esteban, the chief boatman – last impressions of people, last contact with friends.

Bendela was coming around in his racing dinghy. *Tethys,* heeled over, forged steadily ahead, bent on her laborious task. She was not to know any rest for eighty-four days.

I looked at my wristwatch. It was four-twenty in the afternoon. I was just passing the outer breakwater. I reached for the log and made the first entry:

Log of yacht *Tethys*
From: Tangier
To: New York
Wind East, Force 5

And in the column Remarks, I noted: "Two reefs in main. A most satisfactory departure."

Dusk was falling when Cape Spartel came abeam and stood out to the west into the open Atlantic. The easterly wind kept strong. *Tethys,* a famous runner, boiled along, rejoicing in the freedom which at last was ours.

The tide was still with me. By midnight when the wind tapered off, I had put a comfortable distance between the coast and me. From now on, there were not to be any more all night-sessions at the helm. With a passage of such magnitude ahead, it would have been most unwise to waste effort in trying to gain a few miles and squander one's strength and health by endless hours of most unpleasant vigil on deck. At the very start, then, I adopted a steady routine of the voyage: a sound all-night sleep. I never regretted this decision.

Just before leaving I had telephoned the airport for the latest weather reports. "A strong northeasterly right down to the latitude of the Canaries." The officer on duty was most emphatic on this point.

Coming on deck at dawn, I was surprised to find the sea flat as a pancake and *Tethys* pointing east, showing her tail to the very light westerly breeze, as if unwilling to part with her native Mediterranean.

By early afternoon that first day, I was riding out a mild

southwesterly gale under short canvas. It rained, and the sea was quite unpleasant. After three weeks in Gibraltar and nearly a month in Tangier, I felt squeamish, sleepy and without appetite. *Tethys* made slow progress in a general westerly direction. There was nothing I could do on deck, so I spent my time below tucked in my comfortable bunk, digging into the pile of magazines. At night I carried the weatherproof kerosene lamp and tied it to the boom gallows. Through the sliding hatch I could see the light dancing on the cream-painted boom, a reassuring sight.

For four long days the weather continued rainy, the wind irregular. It would shift between south and west. I let *Tethys* choose her own way and patiently awaited the change.

For the first thousand miles my general course was to be southwest. The extreme southerly point to the whole trip was to be decided by the trade winds. Naturally, I was eager to sail the shortest possible route, descending towards the south the very minimum necessary. Even so, I could not hope to keep very much above the twenty-second degree of latitude north. Westing was what I really needed. New York, my destination, lay just below the forty-first degree.

I spent long hours over the charts speculating as to the best course. I used one general Atlantic chart, a French chart, two British charts of the western and eastern parts and American pilot charts which show winds and currents for each month of the year. In my mind, I was sure of one thing: I was not going to beat against the wind. I was going to go and look for a fair wind. I was going to follow the wind.

Nothing is eternal in this world. The contrary wind blew its strength out finally. It gradually went to the west-northwest, and then suddenly jumped to the northeast where it really belonged at that time of the year. On April 16 I had all the wind I needed – and more! The northerly swell rose to majestic proportions. I was off at last!

At sea I find it difficult to measure the passage of time the way it is done on land. There are no office hours, no appointments to keep, no letters to write, no trains to catch, no holidays or weekends. It is done in an entirely different manner, especially on a deep-sea passage. Naturally the days have to be ticked off most carefully. To lose the date would be disastrous, for it would no longer be possible to navigate. It was, therefore, my habit first thing in the morning to mark the day in the nautical almanac and write the date and the day of the week in the ship's log. This way I was assured of keeping track of the calendar passage of time, as it were.

The actual physical sense of the time going by is better felt by the distance run and the position on the chart. Many deep-water sailors when far from land do not bother to plot the position each day. I made it a point to note the daily run and fix the ship's position, the longitude and latitude, each noon. I used, of course, sun fixes for this purpose. It was quite sufficient, and I never felt it necessary to refer to the stars. Once or twice I shot the moon, more for fun than anything else.

As the voyage progressed I became less and less conscious of individual days. It was difficult, nay, impossible to recall the occurrences of each day. I began to remember certain periods, certain very definite groups of days, or weeks, which by similarity of conditions blended into units of time and stood out clearly in my memory. There also were certain incidents, which because of their individual importance stood out all by themselves. However, I remember them as having happened so many days or weeks out of Tangier. It is not difficult to understand, for the importance of meeting a ship two days out cannot be compared with a meeting at sea when one has been alone for fifty-two days. Thus, a very curious encounter occurred at the end of my first week at sea.

The brief period of contrary wind was all but forgotten, and for three days or so I had been under headsails only before a strong northeasterly and a long swell, impressive in its height but harmless and easy on the ship. To someone brought up on the Baltic and the Mediterranean where wave formation is short, steep and hard to take even when running, this long, high Atlantic sea was a pure delight. *Tethys* with her greatest beam forward of amidships and a long keel was perfectly suited for these conditions. She kept an absolutely straight course with jib and forestaysail sheeted as flat as possible and the helm free. She required no attention whatsoever, and although she had to keep the wind a little on one quarter, it was good enough for my purpose. In fact, without any self-steering device, she was under better control at all times. That particular morning, the day was sunny and clear. As usual I rose at dawn. After completing the chores and a hearty breakfast, I turned in for a couple of hours of reading. *Tethys* ran at a good four knots, steady on her course. Soon I was engrossed in a mystery story, totally detached from my surroundings.

Suddenly, my relaxed senses were sharply brought to action by an unfamiliar sound. A flapping sail? Impossible. In a split second I knew what it was: a ship's crew dangerously close! Heaving myself out of my bunk, I saw through the open hatch the sight I always dreaded most at sea, the bow of a ship towering over my stern. I was on deck in less than no time. My first thought was "she missed me!" when I saw that her bow was already crossing the stern, cutting my wake at right angle. I looked along her hull and saw her name, *Tourgenef,* then up to her bridge. Many men and women lined the rail. Someone, probably the captain, was shouting to me, "Are you all right?" I waved and shouted back, "Yes, yes, I need nothing at all," and I plunged below for my camera. The captain was still shouting, but our vessels were already drawing away, so I could not make out what he was trying to tell me.

I sat in the cockpit for a long while, weak with excitement. A splendid feat of seamanship to bring a big vessel like her so close to a running boat. But surely it would have been better to call me on deck with the ship's siren like other ships had done back in the Mediterranean. *Tourgenef* was a whaler on her way towards Madera, Spain. The only explanation for her action was that perhaps the captain was unfamiliar with this form of ocean transportation. He must have taken me for a shipwrecked mariner, a fugitive from justice or just a plain lunatic. In any case, I was glad to see her disappear below the western horizon.

*****

The first month at sea I best remember by the exhilaration of the downhill ride before a huge long sea and a wind which was strong and steady. At one point it blew a good thirty knots, and I streamed sixty fathoms of two-inch manila to keep her on course.

I was a little bothered by the overcast sky and lack of sun. The sunlight was about the only thing I really missed. Gray skies have a rather depressing effect on a solitary voyager. Gone are the bright colors and warmth. I also felt cheated out of the two best moments of a day at sea: sunrise and sunset.

By the end of the second week, I was hoping to sight the Canary Islands. I had no intention to call there or even come close to land or make contact with people. Nevertheless, I thought it would be interesting to have even a brief and distant glimpse of these famous islands. I shaped my course to pass within twenty miles of Palma, the westernmost island, but the notoriously bad visibility in these waters and my doubtful D.R. position made me unwilling to look too closely. I went on without sighting land.

On April 27, fifteen days out, I was clear of the Canaries. I settled down to a steady routine of a deep-sea voyage. From then on, there would be no land of any sort for close to three thousand miles. I carried no more light on deck. With the unlimited sea room, I felt safe and comfortable.

It continued to be rather cold and cloudy. I longed for the sun and blue skies. I was still wearing a woolen shirt and sweater or two and slept under a pile of blankets. It was not easy to keep my body clean under such conditions, for the chilly water did not invite any extensive bathing on deck. All I had courage to do was to sponge myself with seawater, then, after a vigorous rubdown with a rough towel, dress warmly and hope for the best. It worked fine.

In fitting out for the trade wind run, I had prepared a rig device used when running dead before the wind. Many deep-sea voyagers have used it with considerable success as it is especially convenient in the trade winds which blow regularly in one direction.

The arrangement consists of two headsails of equal area set flying or hanked on twin forestays, spread outboard on two independent booms with the sheets leading aft through blocks to the tiller. When the boat changes directions, the pressure on the windward sail becomes greater. The sheet acts upon the tiller and brings the boat back on course. Theoretically the boat should keep her course indefinitely. I had the whole bag of tricks on board, and I was eager to try them out.

The day after I passed the Canaries I judged to be just right for setting up the rig. My latitude was just under twenty-seven degrees north. The wind had fallen somewhat, leaving the sea confused. Without steady pressure on her sails, *Tethys* kept unusually lively. It was extremely difficult to work on the jumping foredeck. At times I had to lie flat on deck holding on with my legs while trying to shackle on blocks and reef through the various part of the genoa, which overlaps the mainsail giving power when the wind is towards the beam. For three solid hours I worked, gradually losing my temper, wishing I had not troubled to carry the confounded thing.

When finally everything was ready and I connected the sheets to the tiller, *Tethys* simply refused to obey. She decided she was not going to be harnessed with any contraptions. The twin booms were lifting constantly, the sails collapsing, the boat turning one way or another, refusing to go back on course. In great disgust, I took off the device as speedily as I could manage, and *Tethys* continued happily under her normal rig. The failure of the twin staysails, which incidentally was due entirely to my bad design, forced me to keep steering if I wanted to carry full sail.

At heart I did not regret that I could not use the self-steering arrangement. In planning my voyage, I tried to follow as closely as I could the two previous voyages over the same route, those of Alain Gerbault and Edward Allcard. Of all single-handers, those two I consider to be the greatest of all. Allcard with his four solitary crossings of the Atlantic is, in my opinion, the greatest living solitary sailor. Gerbault's end was tragic, but his circumnavigation of the globe in *Firecrest* which followed the voyage from Gibraltar to New York, will remain a classic of small boat adventure. Neither of them utilized self-steering gear. When Gerbault made his crossing, it was not yet known. Allcard chose, for some reason, not to use it. So now I was on equal footing with them, and I was glad of it.

The first week of May continued gray and sunless. The good northeasterly was fading away. It was obvious that I would have to go further south to look for more wind. On May 8 I made a sharp descent towards the south. The end of my first month at sea saw me nearing the Tropic of Cancer. An entirely new world opened up before my amazed eyes.

One by one appeared all the wonders of the tropical waters. The flying fish came in whole squadrons. The first sight of Portuguese men-of-war caused excitement beyond all imagination. Never would I have believed it possible for a floating piece of jelly-like substance to cause such a rapturous delight. True, the little creatures were grace and beauty of color out of proportion to their primitive structure. I spent a whole morning trying to capture a specimen, and then I kept it on deck in a bucket. Was it mere curiosity or a secret craving for companionship?

Later in the day, two bosun birds appeared, beautiful things but clumsy fliers. It made me feel tired to look at their heavy flapping wings and unsteady flight. When one dove to catch a fish, it looked as if it had collapsed from exhaustion, and I altered course to rescue the unfortunate animal. Yet they must have tremendous endurance those birds. The nearest land, the Cape Verde Islands, were seven hundred miles away, so obviously they did not depend on any steady base. I never saw any of them alight on the sea to rest. They would come each morning keeping up with me and then disappear somewhere before the sun went down. I always had at least two flying around.

With the northeasterly slowly but steadily dying away, the weather became warm, even hot. It was most welcome. Life at sea is so much easier if you can dispense with heavy clothing. It also gave the proper background, if it can be so called, to the tropical latitudes I was now entering. One does expect to swelter under the tropical sun.

The sea was calm, gone were wind waves. The smooth surface of the ocean was disturbed only by a long, gentle swell coming from the northwest, a remnant of heavy weather thousands of miles away.

It was my first experience of calm weather in the Atlantic. Far from being annoyed, I took advantage of it to reorganize my accommodation, re-stow everything, check provisions, dry clothing and blankets, and above all laze on deck soaking in the sun I missed so much in the first weeks of the voyage. In moderate doses, calm is a pleasant change from the constant violent motion. It gives opportunity for rest and generally provides variety which human nature seems to require from time to time.

*****

The fresh linen felt smooth and pleasant to my sun-soaked body. I stretched in my bunk with a deep feeling of contentment. The kerosene lamp illuminated the cabin with a cozy yellow light. The Homer receiver, placed within easy reach, was alive with music coming from somewhere in outer space.

I lay relaxed, pensively surveying my peaceful little world. The sea could be a place of peace. Wasn't the pursuit of adventure also a quest for peace of mind, and through this, the way to happiness? What we all want most in life if not happiness? A permanent state of bliss is, of course, a pure utopia. But there are moments when one does feel happy, almost completely and perfectly happy. This evening was one of those rare moments in life free of desire or longing for anything else.

The day was the 12th of May. The last signs of land had

disappeared over the northeastern horizon nearly a month ago. I was one thousand six hundred sixty miles in the Atlantic and heading west. One-third of my long voyage lay astern.

For a long moment I thought of the events of the day I had just lived. The wind had been much lighter than the first three weeks out. I had devoted most of the morning to cleaning the boat and re-stowing gear and food. I had dried my bread hard and cut it to breakfast pieces with a saw. I still had enough for twenty-eight days.

There was a lot of sun, and I stripped for the first time and basked in the life-giving rays. The ability to live in the present is a great gift. I confess, however, that I have not yet acquired that quality. It is not difficult to enjoy a particularly pleasant experience for a short while. But I cannot exist just in the present moment. Sooner or later my thoughts go to the future or the past. You can imagine the future as you would want to have it. The past, well, that cannot be changed. It is possible, though, to conveniently forget the nasty moments and think only of the happiness you have lived. It is one of the better sides of human nature to forget the hardships, failures, injustice and malice of other people. All these dissolve as time goes by, leaving only the memory of success and satisfaction.

My immediate future lay traced in a long curved line on the chart of the vast Atlantic. The day-by-day progress of my life was marked there. Nowhere else is a man more master of his destiny than at sea alone. I have a very strong belief in God, but I am also deeply convinced of man's free will, God's gift. Providence never refuses guidance, leaving us freedom in our decisions, freedom to choose the course of our lives.

I became conscious that music had stopped, possibly for station identification. Yes, there it was: Radio Africa in Tangier, a link with the past so distant now and yet so vivid and alive in my mind.

CHAPTER TWELVE

Two days later the trade winds were back, and I began the race towards the halfway mark of the voyage.

I was aiming to reach this imaginary line on the fortieth day out. If I succeeded, it would mean I stood a good chance of completing the passage in eighty days flat, for I had no reason to doubt that the second half could be covered in a similar lapse of time. My prognosis proved to be in both cases near the mark.

During the following five days, I covered more than four hundred miles. An ocean racing man will smile with pity at such a distance. But let's make a little comparison. I once saw a photograph of a forty-six-foot racing sloop, not a big yacht by any standards, and yet her crew numbered nine men, none of them weighing under two hundred pounds. She must have had, I imagine, at least eighteen different sails on board. Her initial cost and her equipment were probably worth a hundred thousand dollars and her annual upkeep a third of that sum. My boat was twenty-five feet long, and I was alone.

To keep the average I had to steer all day. I followed a simple routine of getting up half an hour before sunrise. I did all the morning chores and prepared my lunch, which usually consisted of a can of vegetables, a can of fruit and coffee. Then, with the sun over the horizon, up would go the mainsail with perhaps a reef or two depending on the strength of the wind.

My navigation tools – the sextant, the altitude and azimuth

tables, nautical almanac, my Seamate Omega watch, which served as chronometer, paper and pencils – were all kept handy. At about eight I would take a sun sight for longitude. As a matter of fact, it would be many sights, which I would then work out, taking the average as my position line. After that, I would get ready for the meridian sight to determine latitude. This never failed to excite me, for by bringing forward my morning longitude and crossing it with the noon latitude, I had a fix, which I plotted on the Atlantic chart and also on the pilot chart. I had then the distance run in the preceding twenty-four hours. I amused myself by adding up the total mileage since the beginning of the voyage and the past week, comparing the calculation with other periods, forecasting for the next day, week and so on. Late in the afternoon with the sun in the west, I usually worked out another longitude line, just as a check on my progress.

I never wore a stitch of clothing right through the day. There really was no need. After a few days of exposure, my skin became brown and impervious even to the strongest vertical sun. Nor did I feel any need to cover my head. I could take, without ill effect, a full day of sunshine. With the passage of time, my hair became thick and of unusual length, affording adequate protection. Nature seems to provide for all.

By the middle of the afternoon, I would begin to think with pleasant anticipation of the coming evening. Precisely at sunset the main would come down and everything was made snug for the night. There would still be twenty minutes of light, a most pleasant part of the tropical day, which usually I spent stretching a little in the cockpit after so many hours of steering. I liked seeing the first stars appear, a wonder of nature that never failed to impress me by its simple beauty.

Down below it felt as if I had come home from a good day's sail, a remarkable sensation. The smell of dinner cooking on the never-failing stove, music, books, peace and quiet. Simple life, simple pleasures, but how very rewarding and how far from the pressures and complexities of life ashore.

May 20 found me within one hundred miles of my halfway

mark. I grew a little impatient with the falling wind and slow progress. My runs the following three days were thirty-four, twenty-eight and twenty-two miles. For the first time since leaving Tangier I felt tinges of restlessness invading my thus far tranquil disposition. A ridiculous feeling, but I began to think of this halfway mark as something tangible, as a goal which must be attained, conquered, put behind me as soon as possible. It was a most unreasonable and childish attitude towards a problem which really did not exist. It was only a creation of my imagination. For hours I stared at the line I traced across the chart of the Atlantic pondering the vicissitudes of ocean voyaging under sail. I felt defeated. I considered myself a failure. I could hardly think of anything but getting to that invisible boundary. And there was no one to tell me not to be silly, to sit down, have patience and enjoy myself.

Finally, on May 23 at six p.m. ship's time, I sailed across my mark, forty-one days out of Tangier. That night I celebrated in grand style. There was a very special dinner, a cake I had taken for the occasion and the last of Bep's excellent wine. Before leaving Tangier, I gave away all the wine and liquor, keeping only one bottle for precisely this moment. Unconventional as I am in my habits, I could not but conform to the accepted usages. I found it impossible to depart from what I basically consider a primitive and rather barbarous custom. A formal banquet is still and will remain the very highest form of honoring a guest or an occasion. Fine, but when one considers the natural process this food will have to follow, well, it does appear somewhat unaesthetic and silly.

The weather during the last week of May continued calm. Having attained my goal, I no longer felt particular need for speed. The seven days that followed my halfway crossing advanced me little more than two hundred miles. It was to remain the slowest week of the entire voyage. To compensate, though, an event occurred which kept my spirits at an all-time high.

On the night of May 23 the first sounds of the New World came through on my Homer receiver. Station WWL of New

Orleans was on the air, very faint, and no wonder, for it was two thousand five hundred miles away. That same night I also heard British Guiana, Brazil, Venezuela, Trinidad and Montevideo in far-off Uruguay. I stared for a long time with deep admiration at my receiver, a marvel of radio engineering. The transistor radio is truly an ideal contact with the outer world. It is an invaluable instrument to possess on a vessel engaged upon a long-distance voyage. Four batteries no bigger than my little finger saw me safely across an ocean. With an ordinary set, having no way to recharge the batteries, I would have to limit myself to a few minutes of reception a day. With a set like mine, there really was no need to put any restriction on its use.

It might be purely my imagination, but I like to believe that during the prolonged periods of solitude I had developed a sixth sense for feeling the presence of other human beings. It is a very definite sensation, nothing elusive or uncertain about it.

On the afternoon of May 29 a peculiar feeling of not being alone came over me. I had been forty-seven days at sea. It was well over a month since my meeting with the whaler *Tourgenef.*

Careful scanning of the horizon revealed nothing. I went about my business the usual way, but the feeling persisted. I could not shake off the strange impression of having company somewhere near. When darkness came I sat down below to dinner and some reading.

I will never know what made me go back on deck, for I was in the middle of a very tasty dish when I felt a sudden compulsion to go above. I peeped around over the companion hood, and there it was, a steamer's lights not two miles away. Frankly, I half expected it to be there, but still, the sensation was uncanny. For a moment I refused to believe it, that there really existed anything else but the sea, the wind and my lonely boat. I was anxious to make contact, and at the same time I resented the intrusion upon my little world. No, I did not really want to attract attention, but it was definitely getting a little crowded around these parts. The stranger must be warned off. I rushed below, frantically dug out my faithful kerosene lamp, and with trembling hands tried in vain to make it work properly. I broke the glass, I spilled kerosene all over, I burnt my finger, I knocked my head on the companion hatch, and when I finally managed to struggle on deck, my steamer was all but disappearing over the horizon to the southwest.

I often thought of my actions that night without being able to explain them. I suppose one does react rather strangely if removed from conventional surroundings for a long time. There was no need whatsoever for me to show any light.

Next day my noon sight gave me the latitude of twenty-one degrees fifty-six minutes north of the equator, which was to be my southernmost point of the voyage. It became quite difficult to obtain an accurate altitude of the sun for a latitude position, for at noon I had it virtually overhead. In such conditions error of observation is greater than when the sun is low over the horizon.

During this eventful week I ate the last of my onions and potatoes, and one evening I scrambled my last two eggs. From then on I was out of all fresh provisions, for the lemons were long finished. I should definitely have taken more of the four items. However, I did not find out until a week after the departure from Tangier that potatoes in jackets can be cooked in sea water and remain sweet. Until then I always cooked them in fresh water, which is a great waste of this most precious commodity on a long voyage. I started to take one vitamin pill each day to compensate for the lack of fresh provisions, but even so I finally arrived very deficient in vitamins. It did not become apparent till the months following my landing. Generally my health continued normal, and I even managed to put on some weight. This served me well, for in the last stage of the passage I was losing weight at an alarming rate.

A most significant event, but purely of a morale-building nature, was the fact that I had in my position plotting entered the western sheet of the Atlantic Ocean chart. From then on, I was sailing towards a continent and not away from one. Rather then count the miles left astern, I counted the distance to New

York. It was of great importance to me. It was a visible sign of progress, of achievement, of success.

The tropical waters, which I now was sailing, also brought squalls. I was totally unfamiliar with the structure and behavior of this tropical phenomena, and my first experience of it was not too pleasant, but a good lesson nevertheless. For a day or two I saw squall clouds forming over the horizon. It was not difficult to see that only those directly to windward could in any way come near my boat. For two days I managed to avoid them. On the third day a big wide squall formed directly to windward, and I decided to run before it. It was not moving with any particular speed. I judged that there could not possibly be much weight in it. A sad mistake, that.

As usual, I sat in the cockpit with nothing on. The prospect of a fresh-water shower seemed most attractive, having had no such luxury for nearly fifty days. When the wind struck, I paid out the mainsheet and let her run before it. At the beginning the streams of rain on my salt-covered body felt cool and pleasant. For twenty minutes I drove on with wind increasing and water pouring in torrents. I had no choice but to drive on. There was no question of rounding up or dropping the main as I went. I had to keep her dead before the wind. After half an hour it became bitterly cold and I started to shiver violently. Another ten minutes went by without any sign of the wind wanting to slack off. I felt most uncomfortable. Then, quite suddenly, I was out of it. After that I was more careful. In fact, I became quite timid and many a time lowered the mainsail for nothing.

The following day or two are rather difficult to place in my mind. I have a vague recollection of a period totally different from what I knew till then. The prevailing light gray and blue tones in which I lived for so many weeks gave way to depressing blackness and shades of dark gray. Clouds were heavy around the horizon. The water as far as my eyes could reach was black and menacing. Even the few fish, motionless, were black. I felt as if I had entered some mysterious, prehistoric primitive world. But above all, the sense of so much emptiness was hard to endure.

The silence was almost complete, the ticking of my cabin clock defying the time which seemed to stand still. Looking back at this period I often wonder whether it was real or just a dream.

*****

June 1, my fiftieth day at sea, was ushered in by the most violent squall so far. I came near losing my sails and perhaps my mast too. The night before there was a faint breeze from the north-northeast. I left *Tethys* for the night under all sail with the main boom squared all out. Around two a.m. a dead calm set in. The light rain increased to a formidable downpour. I should have gone on deck to take off the main, but it was pitch black and wet out there, so I fell asleep instead.

It must have been some hours later when I woke up to a screaming squall, the ship on her ends. Glancing at the compass, I jumped on deck. I saw she was heading east, hove down by a northerly blow. It took a full hour to drag the mainsail on board and another hour to make her snug. When she was reduced to a storm forestaysail only, the wind began to taper off. At daybreak there was hardly a breeze left. An hour later she was under full sail again, the wind in the southerly sector. I was a much wiser man after this experience.

The outburst was the last unsettled weather in that latitude. Next day the wind set in from the east-northeast. In the following fifteen days I covered one thousand sixty-six miles, all the time running before a fair wind, varying in direction between northeast and southeast.

Life is so arranged that for each unpleasant experience something invariably occurs to compensate for it. My night squall was rewarded by the most delightful meeting I ever had at sea. It came at the end of a perfect day on June 3. At midday I had noted a run of eight-seven miles from the previous noon. The breeze was strong but *Tethys,* with one reef in her main, was a joy to steer. I was well rested and in a most optimistic mood.

On that occasion I did not anticipate company, and the

approach of the big tanker took me by surprise. I was steering into the sunset, the brilliant path attracting all my attention when, looking over my shoulder, I saw the big ship a mile to windward and changing course to bear down on me.

This time I took it calmly. There was no rushing about. I prepared my camera, I hoisted the ensign, then I jibed her to come close to the oncoming ship. By the time I was ready, she was close astern of *Tethys* passing on to windward. I did not try to stop her or make any signals. I waved a greeting and took some photos. People on her bridge were waving back. She rushed past without reducing speed, her high wash came on me. *Tethys* rolled and pitched violently. Her name was *Arca*. She was a Shell tanker on her way to Venezuela or Trinidad. I was then fifty-two days out, but I stuck to my principle of not trying to pass any signals. I needed nothing. I was flattered to be taken for a deep-sea ship which did not require anything from anybody. I have little sympathy for people who put to sea in badly found vessels and become a nuisance to others. I did not even exhibit my vessel's name on the canvas dodger as is so often done. I would have considered such a thing too much of self-advertising. Altogether a delightful and satisfying meeting at sea.

Next day I began to shape my course towards the northwest. The recommended route for sailing vessels is to reach a position of longitude fifty-nine degrees and latitude twenty degrees north, and from there sail on a northwesterly course to longitude seventy degrees. My progress promised to be so good that I decided to cut corners and make a much tighter circle nearer Bermuda. The days that followed were amongst the best of any sailing I have done before or since. The weather was very steady and the wind fair, although it varied constantly between northeast and southeast. I had all the sun I wanted, and the sea kept small.

The ideal conditions gave me ample time to meditate on this business of ocean voyaging in small sailing vessels. I never tired of recalling in my mind the many voyages I read of and the small boat sailors I have met.

The West Indian islands lay to the southwest five hundred miles away. I no longer felt any temptation to see them. They would have to be the subject of another voyage. Now my goal was New York.

CHAPTER THIRTEEN

For some reason, perhaps because his was the first book I ever read on small boat deep-sea sailing, Alain Gerbault had always been the ideal I secretly tried to emulate. There is about him a romance and mystery which I think no other single-hander has ever attained. He was, as the French have called him, the most solitary of all single-handers. At the age of twenty-nine, after a brilliant career as a flyer in the French Air Force in the 1914-18 war, Gerbault set out from Gibraltar in 1923 in his thirty-nine-foot gaff cutter *Firecrest*. He completed the passage to New York in one hundred one days. A year later after having converted his boat to a Bermudan rig, he continued alone around the world, finishing the voyage in 1929. By then he had decided to spend the rest of his life in the South Pacific. Apparently, he had fallen in love with Polynesia and its inhabitants. He left France again in 1932 for his beloved South Seas. This time his ship, which he called after himself, *Alain Gerbault*, was specially built to his own design, an extra strong, thirty-four-foot double-ender, but not unlike a Norwegian Colin Archer. Gerbault remained in the Pacific until his tragic death in Timor in December 1941. He never established a home on land and never married. His life was entirely devoted to improvement of living conditions of the Polynesians. He advocated the return of old customs and habits. His great ambition was to write the history of the Polynesian peoples, until then passed on only as legends. Most unfortunately, his precious manuscripts were lost together with his boat following his death and the Japanese invasion of Timor.

Here then was a man who succeeded in maintaining life at sea for nearly twenty years. His literary output was prodigious. He wrote seven books of which I think "In Quest of the Sun" is by far the best. There are also at least three books written about him.

Joshua Slocum's around the world voyage in *Spray* is perhaps the best known of all such journeys. It has been acclaimed as the greatest sea voyage ever. No doubt Slocum was a great seaman, and he will forever remain the first man to have circumnavigated the world alone. Yet his adventure fails utterly to excite me. I take off my hat to his tremendous feat of seamanship which possibly will never be equaled. I also wish I could meet my end the way he did: disappearing at sea. Still I cannot see the romance in his voyage. Perhaps there is in it a touch of professionalism which I dislike, or maybe the ship has something to do with it, for *Spray* has never been in my eyes the ideal vessel for a single-hander, notwithstanding the fact that no fewer than two dozen boats on her lines have been built in the pasty fifty years. Or perhaps it is simply because Slocum does not impress me as a romantic figure. Gerbault was a sportsman and a gentleman sailor, an idealist. Slocum was a professional in the game.

Harry Pidgeon certainly deserves recognition for his two voyages around the world alone, although I never admired his hard-chine *Islander*. To me the beauty of the sailing ship is the essential part of going to sea. There are ships to which I feel instantly attracted, and there are others which leave me cold. Ships are like women, only more so.

Pidgeon was one of those rare people who succeeded in making small boat deep-sea sailing a lifelong project. But he entered the field rather late in life – he was over fifty – and knew well what he was after. His extremely simple tastes made him ideally suited for life at sea, where material comforts are few and hardships numerous, but there is freedom galore, freedom virtually unknown in any other ways of life.

Vito Dumas, an Argentinian, I admire for his toughness and singleness of purpose. His voyage alone around the world in the roaring forties will possibly never be repeated. His was a record-breaking enterprise: the eleven months he took to complete the circuit is the fastest voyage ever made by one man. Starting from Buenos Aires and sailing east, he only made three stops, in South Africa, New Zealand and Chile. His ship, the ketch *Lehg II,* was well suited for such a tough test, but the credit must go entirely to the man who was capable of enduring the extreme conditions encountered below the fortieth parallel of south latitude.

The adventure at sea in grand old style – monstrous waves, howling winds, weeks and weeks of hard driving – is not, I admit, without a certain attraction. But the job calls for men of qualities rarely found nowadays. I for one could never find sufficient stamina, determination, will, or let's speak bluntly, plain guts. The sea in its fury is a terrifying sight to behold which calls for nerves much steadier than mine. Give me the tropical waters any time. The hot sun, the moonlit nights, the steady trade wind and a good sheltered, peaceful haven now and again, and I will be happy!

Charles Violet of the *Nova Espero* is an entirely different type of sailor. I hasten to say that his voyages are amongst my favorite ones. I also have a very particular liking for his boat. She is one of the smallest to have ever gone deep-sea. She is not even pretty. Yet I see in her a beauty and charm difficult to resist. The little yawl is only twenty feet long, her freeboard is far too low, her cabin too high. I had met Charles Violet one November afternoon in 1952 in San Remo, Italy. I was then preparing a voyage that eventually failed. Violet was on his way to England after a circuit of Sicily and a call in Tunisia, Sardinia and Corsica. We became friends during the two weeks he stayed in that delightful Italian harbor. I never tired of listening to the tales of his adventures during his trans-Atlantic passage in the *Nova* with Stanley Smith from London to New York via the Azores and Nova Scotia in the spring and summer of 1951, a mighty voyage of seventy-four days.

Looking from the distance of years at the three voyages of Charles Violet – he made a second single-handed trip to the Mediterranean – it is not the Atlantic saga which excites my imagination. It is his voyage to the blue Mediterranean that my thoughts go often with a feeling of nostalgia. It is perhaps because he sailed the seas I love so much? Closing my eyes I can recall with uncanny vividness the summer calm on the coast of Africa, the yellow cliffs of Malta, the rugged shores of Sicily, the beautiful coast of north Italy, and the winds of that inland sea – the mistral, the sirocco, the gregale, the poniente, the Levanter and so many others. But I cannot help feeling that the real reason lies much deeper. I had met Violet during a particularly difficult period of my life, at a time when my soul was crying for adventure, when each fiber of my body was longing to live this wonderful experience of a deep-sea voyage. I was then engaged in preparing a cruise but already chances of ever getting away were slim. I was tied up in San Remo, unable to make a move in any direction. It was late November 1952 when Violet came to San Remo, a free man, engaged upon an adventurous voyage. In him I saw the embodiment of a deep-sea sailor. I admired him and envied him. He also gave me courage, for he was a visible example, proof that with persistence dreams can come true. His boat was small, his resources slender, his health precarious and yet he carried on.

What finally became of him I know not. Two years after we met, he published a book called "Solitary Journey," a great favorite of mine. Many years later I heard he was selling his share of *Nova Espero.* Perhaps he was giving up the life at sea? If so, I like to think that his many voyages gave him what he was after. I hope he found the answer to his problems. Peace of mind? Happiness?

Meanwhile, *Tethys* drove on, under my guidance by day, alone at night. One late afternoon while washing dishes on deck, I leaned over the side with a pot in one hand and a nylon brush in the other. I made a clumsy movement and the brush, my beautiful red brush, slipped through my fingers and was gone. I jumped to my feet driven by a strong impulse to dive overboard. A very dangerous reaction, but I felt as if I had lost a dear friend. I was so deeply attached to that wonderful red brush, beautifully shaped, with lovely white bristles. The evening was spoiled. I was despondent and also worried by my bizarre feeling.

I mention this trivial incident to illustrate the state of mind one can reach after a prolonged solitude. My loneliness was self-imposed. I had freedom, the wind, sun and glorious sea around me and a good ship under my feet. I shudder to think what a solitary confinement can do to a man's mind when given as punishment.

*****

Wanderlust. The compulsion to travel, to move. Is that an essential component in the structure of a deep-sea sailor?

Baron Hans de Meiss-Teuffen recorded his adventures in a book entitled "Wanderlust." He traveled extensively in Africa for many years. The war saw him performing a highly dangerous job of espionage for the Allies. Immediately after, he was off on a voyage across the Atlantic in the thirty-four-foot yawl *Speranza*. He started in London, reached Casablanca in Morocco, and from there he departed for America. Fifty-eight days later he dropped anchor near New London, Connecticut, a most remarkable accomplishment.

My interpretation of this voyage is that Meiss-Teuffen is basically a traveler and a rover. His Atlantic passage is more a result of the compulsion to move than the dedication to ships and ocean voyaging. Lacking here is the singleness of purpose, the vocation which characterizes those who go to sea in big ships or small, for pleasure or livelihood. It was more, in my opinion, a wish to add one more adventure to a list of other spectacular ones. What I say here is in no way an attempt to belittle the achievement. Very much to the contrary, Meiss-Teuffen stands out as a man of tremendous willpower, courage and resourcefulness.

An excellent example of response to the deep-sea urge, more popularly known as the call of the sea, is the marvelous voyage of the Belgian ketch *Omoo* which went around the world in two years. Annie and Louis Van de Wiele and a friend circumnavigated the globe in their forty-six-foot vessel in what I would term the best yachting style. I know of no other expedition better prepared and executed. Nothing went wrong, ever. Passages were good and fast, and they visited many interesting places. The Van de Wieles took great pride in *Omoo*, and she was a beauty. I had the occasion to meet them in Tunis in 1956. They were beginning a voyage which would take them around Africa. We spent a delightful two days on board and also visiting the ruins of Carthage.

There was no news from them for a long time. Then, one day, I heard they had sold the ship at Mombasa, East Africa, and established themselves in big game safari business!

It must have been a case of sea fatigue. It is very, very difficult to maintain life at sea continuously. Almost invariably, a time comes when even the most devoted feel the need of a prolonged spell ashore.

But the very latest is that they are going back to sea.

*****

A good example of a scientific or experimental approach to deep-sea voyaging is the famous Atlantic crossing of Patrick Ellam and Colin Mudie in the twenty-foot *Sopranino* in 1951 and '52.

This remarkable little cutter was taken on a momentous voyage that began in England and finished in New York, Ellam and Mudie having sailed five thousand miles via the Canary Islands and the West Indies. Both were experienced small boat sailors, and Ellam had collaborated with Lauren Giles on the design of *Sopranino,* created as a miniature ocean racer. The voyage was undertaken with a view of proving beyond all doubt the seagoing qualities of the little ship.

Patrick Ellam eventually brought *Sopranino* alone to New York in the dead of winter. Colin Mudie became famous as a member of the free balloon Small World expedition. I was to meet Ellam on the day of my docking at the 79th Street Yacht Basin in New York. A remarkable man.

I often like to think about the voyage of the *Tai-Mo-Shen* which was made in what I think was the golden age of long-distance voyaging in sailing yachts, the early thirties.

Five young British naval officers stationed in China, of whom Lieutenant Commander Martyn Sherwood was the senior and who subsequently wrote the book "The Voyage of the *Tai-Mo-Shan,*" got together to sail via the north Pacific and the Panama Canal to England. The fifty-four-foot ketch was built for them at Hong Kong, and she had no engine.

The British Navy gave them a year's leave on half-pay, thus making it possible for the five young men to live their adventure. The principal danger in an enterprise of this kind is the breaking up of the ship's company. *Tai-Mo-Shan*'s crew, however, weathered successfully the hardships of each other's company for nearly a year, and the voyage was completed in the best tradition of the sea. To be sure, the Navy was well repaid, for all of them served with great distinction in World War II.

In Sherwood's book, there is a picture captioned "A heavy sea north of Japan." It was taken amidship looking aft. *Tai-Mo-Shan* is sliding down a big roller. Looking at this picture, I can visualize the conditions, the atmosphere of that day. I can feel the moment that happened almost three decades ago. I can feel the adventure. I live it vicariously each time I take Martyn Sherwood's book in hand.

But the voyage my mind went to more often than to any other was Edward Allcard's solo crossing of the Atlantic, in whose wake I was now sailing. He is no doubt the greatest of living single-handers and, I think, surpasses Alain Gerbault by his extremely well balanced and pleasant personality. Gerbault tended to become a misanthrope in the last years of his life.

Allcard liked people and got along well with those around him, though perhaps he did feel a little lonely at times.

Tethys drove on, carrying me on my adventure, untired, faithful, reliable and never resting.

CHAPTER FOURTEEN

The beginning of my third month at sea saw me approaching the end of the trade wind run.

I had reached the longitude of sixty-three and a half degrees west in latitude of twenty-six degrees, the northern limit of the northeast trades. Astern lay three thousand three hundred eighty miles. New York was to the northwest twelve hundred miles away.

But the short distance left gave me little comfort, for I knew that the next eight hundred miles were going to be difficult. I had to go through the horse latitudes, a region of calm, squalls and variable winds. Beyond that lay the Gulf Stream with its strong current, fogs, humidity and squally weather.

Some two hundred miles south of Bermuda I was struck by a short but fairly violent gale. The signs of the approaching bad weather were visible. I had ample time to prepare the ship and myself. With the mainsail off, *Tethys* is easy for one man to handle. Her small headsails are fitted with downhauls, and there are permanent gaskets on the bowsprit and the staysail boom to secure the furled sails.

When the wind increased, I put her to run before it, heading east of north. That way I could do some northing and feel I was getting nearer to New York.

At three in the morning it was blowing a full gale, force eight. I took in the jib and ran under her forestaysail. Two hours later I replaced the jib with the storm jib, a sail of only fifteen square feet of stout canvas, roped all around. The sea got up, but there was no real danger in it. *Tethys* continued running, hardly taking any spray on board. It was now gusting force nine, but I continued to run in perfect safety. In the Mediterranean the seas would have already been breaking. Here in the wide Atlantic it took much longer to whip them up to that state.

Towards dawn it started to rain. After an hour of the heaviest downpour I have ever seen on land or sea, the wind dropped to a mere fresh breeze. It was the end of the storm, once more proving that if there is wind before rain you will soon make sail again.

I had a mixed feeling of relief and regret that the storm was gone so soon. Quite naturally, I am always glad to see the end of bad weather, but at the same time it had long been my desire to live through a full Atlantic storm. I was eager to compare it with the extreme knockdown conditions I experienced in the Mediterranean, and I had unlimited faith in my ship. Storm seas, with great masses of water built up to mountains and valleys, alive and moving, have a fascination which must be experienced to be believed.

The blow was all over on June 20, and again I steered west and then northwest.

Radio Bermuda kept me company in this desolate stretch of water. The island, too, experienced rains and heavy weather. For several days I tuned in to the station. It was strange to come so close, take part in the lives and problems of the offshore island and then hear them fade away, lost in the distance. From there on, America boomed on the air unchallenged by any other station.

My seventieth day at sea found me on the southern edge of the Gulf Stream. In spite of lost time in the gale, I still hoped to complete the passage in under eighty days. The weather became calm, humid, and a little unpleasant. I was also feeling the effects of solitude. I talked to myself regularly, I was losing weight, and I had no appetite. I lived mainly on fruit and vegetable juices. Nevertheless, I felt well physically, and very healthy. After all, there are no germs at sea.

I decided to run with the stream a little, but after a day it set me some eighty miles to the northeast. I had to work my way back towards the west. By the last day of June, I had crossed the stream. New York lay now two hundred miles to the north-northwest. The nearest land was a hundred miles off due west from me.

On the morning of the seventy-fifth day, I fished out of the ocean a cardboard milk container of the National Dairy Products Corporation of Washington, D.C.

It was a thrill, and as good as if I taken a bearing. Land was still well over a hundred miles away, but I could smell hay and dry earth in the evening breeze. The flies, driven by the southwesterly airs, came on board. Butterflies and mosquitoes followed. It was terribly humid and sticky. The balmy, blue days in the fabulous trade winds were gone. This was an unpleasant appendix. I was anxious to end the passage.

I crossed the Philadelphia shipping lane in fog. Many ships came near. They were invisible. Only the bellowing of their sirens, throbbing of the engines and the smell of exhaust fumes signaled their presence. Land was hidden in haze. There was no hope of seeing anything until nightfall when complete darkness would show the loom of shore lights. Meanwhile, the wind had gone to the north and become quite strong. I reduced sail, leaving the ship on the inshore tack.

When I came up on deck at two in the morning, the lights of Atlantic City were clearly visible twenty miles to the northwest. I put her about, heading to sea. It was pointless to go any nearer.

Next day dawned calm and hazy. It was Friday, July 8, my eighty-second day at sea. Small boats were heading out for a day's fishing. I lay becalmed, waiting and impatient.

Early in the afternoon I spoke to a sport-fishing cruiser, the *Mutually Yours*, with Tom Finley and a friend on board. They kindly agreed to telephone a message to New York. I found it difficult to talk. I spoke slowly to appear relaxed and at ease. I was far from that.

A faint breeze sprang up. I headed north along the coast,

not more than five miles distant. The shoreline was invisible at times, hidden in the thick haze, but there was constant humming of automobile engines coming clear over the calm sea.

I kept the radio going, absorbing the sounds of the New World. I was urged to see my Chevrolet dealer today; I was invited to have a real cigarette, a Camel; I learned that Coca-Cola refreshes me best, but that I must be sociable and have a Pepsi; I was informed repeatedly that Bon Ami hadn't scratched yet. I was puzzled. Every two minutes I was told the time and then would come a tune I'd heard hardly thirty minutes before. It was the weekend of the Fourth of July. Motorists were urged to drive with care. Many hundreds of deaths on the road were anticipated. There was no mistake. I was nearing land and all its dangers.

July 5 came and with it the end of my long journey. At seven twenty a.m. I was abeam of Sandy Hook, becalmed. At ten I hailed a Coast Guard cutter requesting a tow.

At noon we docked at the quarantine, eighty-four days out of Tangier, seven months and twenty-eight days out of Tunis. Health and Immigration Authorities were on the pier to greet me. Someone said, "Welcome to America." I felt a quiet pride in a voyage well done.

EPILOGUE

The American authorities, press and public gave me a wonderful reception. The day following my arrival I was towed to the 79th Street Yacht Basin on the Hudson River where the Consul General of Tunisia welcomed me officially as the first Tunisian ship ever to reach America.

A few days after I went to stay with my friend Jean Lacombe, I sold *Tethys* to a young Frenchman living in New York.

Mark learned through the press of my arrival and got in touch with me. He had come over to America by air in May and was staying with friends in Vermont. I found out that I was no longer married to Marina. We had agreed to separate, and the divorce went through while I was at sea. She had married again and was in India with her husband who was doing a job for the American Department of Commerce in New Delhi.

I traveled a little. I saw Mark in Vermont and my parents in Washington where they were visiting with my sister Daisy. In autumn I went to Gloucester to fish out of that famous port.

I felt lost and out of place. I also felt a sea weariness that troubled me greatly. There was in me a sense of great loss which seemed impossible to replace. I had begun to believe what Bertrand Russell said of happiness, that "to be without some of the things you want is an indispensable part of happiness." My dream came true and was no longer there. There was an overwhelming finality about the end of my voyage which I found difficult to accept. I discovered with dismay that I was tired of small boats. It worried me greatly. I knew only time could cure it.

The Gloucester fishing proved to be a boring, cold and unrewarding experience. The days of the large schooners were gone. The adventure was no longer there, only the tedious, hard, gray, never-ending fight for existence.

Christmas came, my first in America. Mark arrived from school in Maryland. We spent several happy days as guests of friends, Harold and Beverly Xavier, just outside Gloucester.

Then it was again time to say good-bye. Mark returned to school. I flew to the West Indies to join the hundred-ten-foot schooner *Le Voyageur.*

For five months I sailed the Windward Islands from Barbados and Grenada to Antigua. Five eventful months.

I met Alfred and Marjorie Petersen in their *Stornoway* and Edward Allcard in the *Sea Wanderer.* I visited many yachts, ports and islands, but I was always glad to come back to the spacious decks of *Le Voyageur* and her ship's company. There was comfort in companionship. We were at times as many as eighteen on board. My job as first mate was pleasant. I all but forgot the sea weariness of my Atlantic voyage. I was ready for more.

At the end of the charter season in May, I took over the fifty-six-foot steel gaff schooner *Oronsay* then lying at Martinique. A few weeks later, I sailed her on a direct sixteen-day passage to New York. Mark came as mate and did extremely well. When autumn came, I took *Oronsay,* now called *Caroline,* to the Virgin Islands. We sailed her again between Barbados and Antigua, the waters I like best.

It is early June 1961 as I write this. Shortly, Mark will come join the ship as mate again. We shall do some cruising. Then he will go back to New York and on to France where his mother is. After two years at the Junior Naval School in Maryland, he had decided to make the Navy his career.

And of the people who appear in my story? Bep Patti is

building a thirty-three-foot yawl in Tunisia and is planning some long-distance trips. Bob Shea has left the American School in Tangier and is reading for another degree at Columbia University. I saw Ron and Evelyn Rohner a week after my arrival in New York where they had come in by air. Now they are in San Francisco where Ron has just received his master's degree in anthropology. Dr. Hans Lindemann, after three Atlantic adventures, is through with the sea, he told me in New York. He will settle down in Hamburg, Germany, to practice medicine.

And what of the future? Well, who can tell what the future will bring? Still, we can all plan and hope. Very definitely, I have decided to make my life at sea, to maintain the seafaring way of life. I know what I want and what I am after. Do I plan any more long voyages? Yes. I have several precise projects: the Mediterranean again, the Island of Fernando Po in the Gulf of Guinea, the Canaries and Cape Verde Islands, the Galapagos and the West Coast of South America. The Caribbean will be my base. Enough is here to keep me busy for many years.

It is doubtful, though, that I shall want to cruise alone again. The gift of friendship and companionship is too precious to waste, and I think I have found a mate to share my adventures.

My ideas of the ship I need are well crystallized. *Caroline,* with her fifty-six feet and the heavy gaff rig, is too large to handle in comfort and needs at least three to sail her. I should like to have a schooner rig. I recognize that a ketch is handier, but who can resist the romance of a schooner. She should be about forty feet long on deck with ample beam, moderate draft, very strong and comfortable at sea, and easily handled by one only, if need be. Her auxiliary power will have to be a diesel, reliable and simple to maintain. With such a ship, there is no limit to one's horizons.

Before departing for the Caribbean I went to say good-bye. to *Tethys.* She was laid up for winter in a quiet berth at Glen Cove, Long Island. She looked very small, abandoned and, I thought, unhappy. Possibly she was dreaming of the dazzling days in the sparkling trades. A faithful little ship, a friend.

Advice to Parents of Adventure Dreamers

Let them go!

If you have a youngster who spends his time dreaming of a sea voyage, let him go. And I will say more: help him. What I write here is based on my own experience. In my young days I had no one around me who understood this. I was born and raised until my teens in an environment totally removed from things maritime. But I happened to have been born with a passion for adventure and deep-sea voyaging. Where it came from I know not. It certainly cannot be hereditary. Amongst my ancestors, there were generals, but as far as I know, no admirals or explorers. I can hardly be blamed for it. Basically, there is nothing wrong with it. We all have this urge for adventure in us to a greater or lesser degree. The thirst is so powerful and natural that in my opinion there is no other cure for it but complete satisfaction. To repress a healthy desire for adventure in a youngster can have a most undesirable effect on his later life.

The best time for adventure is when you are young. At an early age it is easier to combine all the elements necessary to carry out an adventure. Experience and money may be lacking, but a young man will seldom have the attachments and responsibilities we tend to acquire as the years roll by.

If adventure is not lived in early youth, there is the danger that the desire might erupt in later life, sometimes in a most awkward period. Two possibilities will then arise: nature will take its course and the desire for adventure will be fulfilled with ill effects, perhaps, upon the already established life of the individual; or it will be suppressed, creating an unhappy man.

In these few pages I cannot discuss all possible cases as, for instance, when desire for adventure suddenly manifests in an individual who never gave any signs of wanting it before. The Frenchman Paul Gauguin, very late in life left his family in France and simply ran away to the South Seas to become a painter. He was a genius, but he also was an adventurer. Art was his adventure, his way of expression.

A young man's dreams of adventure in most cases are in direct conflict with his education, or rather his formal schooling. His time is spent thinking of blue seas and new horizons. His grades suffer. He is unhappy. His parents are unhappy. This young man should be helped. He should be helped in fulfilling his urge, his instinct for adventure. Suppression of it will not solve his or his parents' problems. If it is only a youthful whim, it will soon be cured. The young man will be back in school and on his way to good grades.

Quite recently I came across a young man who at the age of nineteen simply refused to continue schooling. All he dreamed of was deep-sea ships and adventure. "Education," he would state, "means nothing to me. I love the ships. Sailing is my life." He had grandiose vision of sailing alone around the world. His imagination knew no limits. I must say that he was very good with boats. Considering his age, he knew a lot about them. But he knew nothing about the sea, nor did he know himself.

He was fortunate enough to have been given a chance to buy a good little ship, proven already on many thousands of miles of deep-sea sailing. He prepared the ship beautifully and took off for his life adventure. The result? Fifteen days, six hundred miles and one gale later he was cured. He is back in school and doing nicely. As far as I know, he wants to become a librarian.

The moral of the story is that had he not been given the chance of trying it out, he would have continued on through life with the unhappy feeling of frustrated dreams in his soul, and no education.

I believe that a lot of juvenile delinquency could be eliminated if youngsters with such inclinations could be given a period of six months to two years on board training ships. A program could be developed along these lines. It is, however, outside the scope of this short chapter.

More cautious parents will say, "And what about danger?" My answer is: Of course there is danger, but no more than in any other activity of life. Disasters at sea are rare. Life at sea is clean and healthy. It develops qualities which no land activity can do in the same degree – teamwork, discipline, self-confidence, leadership, appreciation for beauty, a sense of achievement and a better understanding of your fellows. It also develops the ability to accept risks, make decisions and take responsibility for them.

*****

A young man who lives the adventure and completes the task he has set for himself invariably will find his way back home and into school. He will come back more mature, supremely satisfied with his achievement, and better prepared to face life.

Naturally, it will take a while, a year perhaps. Sailing ships are slow. It takes a long time to cross an ocean.

AFTERWORD

I had dinner with my brother Chris in New York shortly after his solitary voyage across the Atlantic. We talked about our childhood. I asked him to go shopping as I wanted to give him a nice present. He laughed and said, "You didn't yet see my boat. It is very small. If you gave me something, I would be obliged to throw something I already have into the ocean to make room."

He was planning to go to Florida to see our sister, Daisy, and make plans for the future. We embraced, my heart ached – I watched his elegant silhouette disappear in the dark street. I was never to see him again.

I loved and admired my brother and I still miss him so.

Countess Astrid de Grabowski Dewart, February 2012

POSTSCRIPT

As the editing of this book neared completion, I returned to Poland and visited for the first time the house where I was born and where my family lived before we fled our homeland in 1939.

I also had the pleasure of spending time with my cousin Marek Zgorniak, an art historian in Krakow, and his family.

I got a big surprise soon after I was back home in Florida when I received from my cousin an e-mail containing a new connection to the final chapter of my brother's life. My cousin shared with me an account he had come across on the Internet about the doomed voyage of the *Enchantress*, written by the grandson of John L. Pelton, the man who had hired Chris to captain his 58-foot schooner. On his website, Collin Pelton, a Los Angeles-based actor, writer and self-described "living descendant of a Bermuda Triangle disappearance", presents his perspective on the tragedy that claimed the lives of his family and of my brother Chris.

Daisy de Grabowski Richardson, August 2012

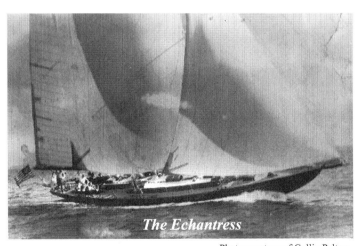

The Echantress

Photo courtesy of Collin Pelton

INDEX

19022125R00101

Made in the USA
Charleston, SC
03 May 2013